All that Glisters

WhoooDoo Mysteries
A division of
Treble Heaat Books

All that Glisters
Copyright © 2011
Don G. Porter
All rights reserved.

Cover layout/design
Copyright 2011 ©Lee Emory
All rights reserved.

WhoooDoo Mysteries
A division of
Treble Heart Books
http://www.trebleheartbooks.com

Printed and Published in the U.S.A.

The characters and events in this book are fictional, and any resemblance to persons, whether living or dead, is strictly coincidental.

All rights reserved. No part of this book may be reproduced or transmitted in any form by any means, electronic or mechanical, including photocopying, recording, scanning to a computer disk, or by any informational storage and retrieval system, without express permission in writing from the publisher.

ISBN: 978-1-936127-89-4
1-936127-89-X
LCCN: 2011943645

***Other WhoooDoo Mysteries
by Don G. Porter***

Gold Fever

(See Mr. Porter's other books on Page 255.)

Chapter 1

"Eight Two Bravo, what's your position?" It was Vickie on the radio, the world's most beautiful and dedicated dispatcher.

"I'm sixty miles out, deadheading back from Tununak. Estimating Tuluksak in forty minutes."

"Forget Tuluksak. You'd better come home."

"What about the passengers? They need to be at the food stamp office before five."

"Pat had a no-show in Aniak so he can pick up Tuluksak on his way down. You just get your tail back here pronto."

That was pretty strong language for Vickie. "Any special reason?" I asked.

"Phone call. It's Renaldo. He's calling from Venezuela every five minutes, and I can't stand to hear a grown man cry."

"Roger. I'll be down in twenty minutes."

I'd been kicking back at five thousand feet, watching about a million birds milling around below me. Fall was coming fast to western Alaska. The tundra had turned from green to russets and golds. The migratory birds that came last spring to nest in the myriad lakes were packing to head south for the winter. White clouds of snow geese wheeled and dived together like schools of fish. Swans, geese, ducks and cranes were practicing their formations and jockeying for positions.

I rolled to a heading for Bethel and trimmed down to lose a couple of hundred feet a minute. The outside thermometer read 45 degrees Fahrenheit, but that would drop fast when the sun went down. The sun was already headed toward the horizon and was going to set a heck of a long ways south of west.

The sky was a perfect blue dome. In Alaska when we say "ceiling and visibility unlimited" we mean it. From 5,000 feet, I could see two hundred miles. The curve of the earth was obvious north, west, and south. Fifty miles east, the Kilbuck Mountains interrupted the horizon. Mt. Hamilton, seventy-five miles northeast, wore a yarmulke of new snow.

The creaky old Cessna 207 I was flying inched up from 155 to 160 knots. It had been a couple of years since I'd heard from Renaldo, and if he was calling, it probably wasn't good. Not that I wasn't happy to hear from him, but when he called, he was usually in trouble.

Renaldo had been my college roommate, so for four years we'd shared the same 12 x 14 cell. We fought and screamed about each other's bad habits, but we went through the rites of passage together. We learned about liquor at the same parties, and about women from the same girls.

In most ways we were opposites. Renaldo was a sharp dresser, a carefully groomed ladies' man. I was more into sports, football in the fall and boxing all winter. We were both business majors, but my electives tended to be whatever was rumored to be easy. Renaldo scrabbled to learn more economics and accounting.

On the occasional evening when there weren't any parties, and Renaldo didn't have a date, we studied at our desks, side by side, looking out over the fields of central Iowa from our third floor window in Gunsolly Hall. We spent more time talking and dreaming than we did reading. Renaldo insisted that he would be a millionaire before he was forty. I did too, but I never believed it. He did. Renaldo hadn't decided on the means yet, but he was focused on the goal.

I already had my student pilot's license at the time. The apex of my dream was captain's bars at Pan American Airlines. Quite a few years have slipped by. There isn't any Pan American Airlines anymore, and I'm a partner in a struggling charter service at the forsaken top of the world.

Renaldo tried a good many different ways to make his million, but every time he had something going, he was slapped down by the slings and arrows of outrageous fortune. He must have offended some personal god, because each time he jumped for a brass ring it turned to pucky in his hand, and he fell on his face. He didn't get discouraged; he just thought of a more extravagant plan and put his heart and soul into it. That was the spirit that had led him to Venezuela a couple of years before to dig shovels full of gold out of a mountain.

Alaska's Yukon/Kuskokwim Delta is flat tundra. From

a few thousand feet it looks like a golf course stretching from horizon to horizon. It's actually moss two feet thick, growing out of silt that's called permafrost. The moss provides insulation, so the ground stays frozen year around. The blueberries and cranberries that give the Eskimos their vitamin C grow in or on the moss, hunkering down to avoid the constant chilling wind.

I was down to two thousand feet, ten minutes from Bethel, when I crossed the Nunapitchuk River. Long, flat, Eskimo boats were tied to willows all along the bank, and the tundra was dotted with big colorful flowers. The flowers were Eskimo women, squatted down, covered by their bright corduroy *kuspuks,* an A-line outer garment that forms a tent when they squat and keeps out the wind, gnats, and mosquitoes.

The women will fill buckets and barrels with berries until the snow falls. The men were out on the Kuskokwim River, drift netting for any fish that were left, and shooting birds by the boatloads for winter meat.

I parked the 207 in front of the gas pumps at Bushmaster Air Alaska, topped off the tanks, and added a quart of oil before I tied it down on the flight line. Full tanks don't collect condensation, but also we always kept the planes ready to go. The next call might be a chain saw accident, someone with a leg half cut off, or maybe someone's hand dangling by a string after he ran it through a boat propeller. A village health aide would be on the radio screaming for an airplane and trying to hold the guy's blood in with her hands.

I hefted my personal flight bag out of the baggage compartment in the nose. The 207 is a 206 stretched longer, and Cessna balanced it by sticking the engine farther out front and putting a baggage compartment between the engine and the firewall. I schlepped the bag into the reception-waiting-ready-room.

Vickie was sitting behind her desk with a phone clamped between her ear and her shoulder. She was in her late-afternoon mode. She came in every morning looking as if she had just stepped out of *Vogue*, but by afternoon a little cloud of honey blonde hair had escaped from her bun. She had a couple of white feathers stuck to her shoulder from something she had helped to load, and she had a tiny smudge of aviation oil on one cheek.

I strolled over to the coffee bar and drizzled a Styrofoam cup full, took a napkin from the bar and went behind the desk. I pointed to her cheek. She took the phone in her hand and tilted her face up. I wiped off the oil and plucked her feathers. Don't get the wrong idea about Vickie. I loved her, of course, and so did everyone else on the Delta, but she was my partner's wife. I loved like Don Quixote, pure and chaste, from afar.

She handed me a slip of paper with a phone number on it. I carried it down the hall to the office to make the call, shoved some overdue bills off the blotter and set the coffee down. Vickie had filled the thirty-cup pot at eight so by four in the afternoon it was wicked. It was hot, though, and I sipped it more from habit than because it was good.

I punched in the numbers from Vicki's note and the phone said, "Hi, Alex, thank heaven you're back."

Renaldo sounded as if he was in the next room instead of a third of the way around the world, the long way. Wonderful things, satellites.

"Hi, Renaldo. What's up?" I used the last seconds available to pretend this was just a friendly call.

All that Glisters // 9

"Alex, Consuela's dead, and I'm next. You've got to get down here."

I didn't ask who Consuela was. I got the general idea from his tone, and if she was dead, I guessed it didn't matter anymore.

"Business problems?" I asked. With Renaldo that was usually the case. I'm not sure how I became his guardian angel; it just grew on us. The first time was in college after a frantic phone call from his girlfriend at an alien frat house. I dashed down there and found Renaldo backed into a corner with three big guys intent on rearranging his face. I grabbed a kitchen chair and waded in. I broke a rung off the chair on every head between me and Renaldo, and Sissy and I lugged him back to our room and patched him up.

His phone calls hadn't all been bad. Sometimes he called when he was riding a new bubble and offering me a partnership in a surefire scheme to mint money. I always went when he called, and I got to see a good bit of the world that way, but the bubbles always broke before I got there.

"Alex, I don't know what's wrong, and I don't know why, but people are getting shot. They shot Consuela because they thought she was me, and they're still trying to kill me. How soon can you get here?"

I noticed he didn't ask if I *could* come, or if I *would* come, just how soon.

"There's a jet leaves for Anchorage in two hours. I'll be on it."

"Meet me in Caracas. You'll land at Maiquetia. Take a taxi to Central Park in Caracas. That's *Parque Centrale*. Got that?"

"Yeah, Central Park, I guess I can find that. Don't you have a street address?"

"Not in Caracas, just districts. Take the Avenue Lecuna a few blocks left to the Plaza Bolivar. I'm staying in the El Conde, registered as John Smith."

"That's good, Renaldo, that's really good. Just a minute while I write that down so I won't forget it. John Smith, how do you spell that?"

"Just hurry." Renaldo hung up.

I replaced the dead phone and took a sip of the coffee. It was definitely stale, and down to lukewarm, but I drank some anyway. I'm too cheap to throw it out. I went back out to the reception desk to tell Vickie there had been a slight change in plans. That's an advantage of being a partner. No pay while I was gone, of course, but my job would be waiting for me.

Vickie scowled and started reblocking the next day's schedule. She's good at that. There might be a plane down with a flat tire at Mountain Village. Vickie would reroute someone from Holy Cross for the passengers, stick a spare tire on the next flight to Emmonak, double up some other flights and keep the people moving right along until the plane was back in the air.

I hefted my flight bag into my locker and unzipped it to take out the .357 magnum. It's the Smith and Wesson patrolman model with a six-inch barrel, touted to be the most powerful and accurate handgun ever made. Mainly I liked it because the grips were small enough to wrap my hand around. I never feel quite in control using the big macho grips on Colts.

I tossed the gun onto the passenger seat of my old International pickup and tooled into town through the tundra on the only six miles of paved road in western Alaska. I passed the familiar spruce tree beside the road halfway to town. It's a little bigger than the average Christmas tree, and the only tree within forty miles if you head east. It's the only tree within two hundred miles if you head north or south. Going west, two hundred miles brings you to the Bering Sea without passing anything you couldn't grow in a flowerpot.

The Bethel city fathers and mothers erected an official-looking sign next to the spruce tree. "You are now entering Bethel National Forest." The "You are now leaving" part is on the other side of the same sign. You have to have a sense of humor to live in Bethel.

I turned off the state highway and took the dirt Main Street and then Front Street to my cabin on the riverbank. The Kuskokwim River behind the cabin was a mile wide, and dark brown, like baker's chocolate. It looked cold, and it was. The water temperature of the Kusko is around 40 degrees in high summer.

Near the middle of September we were getting frosts every night, but no ice running on the river yet. I turned the oil stove in my kitchen/living/dining room up high and checked the water barrel in my bath /utility room. There was half a barrel of water and the hot water tank had enough warm for a shower because the oil heater/cook stove had been on low all day.

I took the shower and turned on the taps in the bathroom and the kitchen sink. All that water gushing down the drain and out into the river strained my miser's soul, because in Bethel water cost six cents a gallon. The water pump ran until the barrel was dry. I shut off the pump at the breaker panel and unscrewed the little plug out of the bottom to drain it. I also pulled the fill spout in through the wall so the city water truck wouldn't fill up the barrel while I was gone. I stuck a rag in the hole through the wall.

Bethel doesn't have running city water because the ground is permanently frozen. Not only would water pipes freeze, but the ground moves around so much it would break buried pipes. The term *frost heave* doesn't begin to describe what happens on the tundra. The city has two fleets of trucks, if three trucks make a fleet. One fleet delivers water, the other picks up honey buckets.

A "honey bucket" is a ten-gallon steel bucket with a good sturdy bale. You build a wooden box around it and mount a toilet seat on the box. Everything you wouldn't want to go into the river goes into the honey bucket, and when the odor becomes offensive, you splash in a cup of Pinesol. The city collects the buckets and hauls the contents out of town to a leaching pond, called Honey Bucket Lake, of course.

The most important survival skill in Bethel is knowing when to put your honey bucket out so it doesn't freeze solid before the truck comes to empty it. You might be wrinkling your nose and thinking "how primitive," but remember you're a member of only the second or third generation in the history of the world to just flush things away.

Every time you flush a toilet, you use a few gallons of good potable water. If a shortage of drinking water ever threatens civilization, we may see honey buckets lining the streets of New York, again.

I packed two suitcases and field stripped the .357. The frame went into one bag and the cylinder and a box of Remington copper clads in the other. That made it pretty legal as checked baggage in most places. I noticed that I had just packed a parka. I took it out of the suitcase and hung it in the closet, I had a feeling I wouldn't need it in Venezuela.

All that Glisters // 13

I scooped the perishables out of the refrigerator into a cardboard box. My next-door neighbor wasn't home, but I opened his front door and shoved the box inside. No need to leave a note. He would correctly interpret the milk and eggs, and glance out the window now and then to see that my cabin hadn't fallen into the river.

I shut off the fuel oil with the valve at the barrel, and pulled the disconnect switch on the breaker box. Might as well let the cabin freeze. If I was gone for over a week, it would freeze anyway, no matter what I tried.

A Wien Airline 737 rushed me to Anchorage at 30,000 feet, but the view of the Alaska Range was still spectacular because the mountains reach half way up to the airplane. The setting sun had turned Mt. Denali into a strawberry sundae. I made a mad dash across the Anchorage airport and skidded onto an Alaska Airlines 727. The view of Prince William Sound and the Wrangell Mountains distracted me from leg cramps for a while. After the second landing, things began to blur. Train rides through tunnels, always from one end of an airport to the other. Escalators long enough to require oxygen masks climbed to gate changes, back to the tunnels, yet a third end to airports, more escalators.

Flight attendants changed uniforms, seats got smaller and lumpier, daylight disappeared in the early afternoon and came back in the middle of the night. Breakfasts were served at dinnertime. Choice was between screaming with leg cramps or climbing over sleeping passengers.

Jets have made impossible things possible, and I appreciate that, but when you're wedged between garlic breath on one side, beer breath on the other, and can't stretch even your fingers properly, it seems the effort, bravery, and stamina required to travel ranks right up there with pushing a Conestoga wagon across the prairie.

Chapter 2

Maiquetia seemed to be in a fog. Not the airport, just me. I collected my two old suitcases and shambled down the wide tiled hallway wondering where to find a taxi. I passed a booth in the lobby that was labeled "Ital Cambio" but looked like American Express. It was obviously in the business of changing currency, and that struck me as a good idea.

I don't have much of a research library in Bethel. I doubt a Wall Street Journal has ever been west of Anchorage, but I do have Webster's Encyclopedic Unabridged Dictionary. Mine was printed in 1998. It's heavy enough to hold glue joints and tells me most things that I want to know. When I checked, my dictionary said that the currency of Venezuela is the Bolivar and the exchange rate is 4.2 Bolivars to the dollar. I handed three twenty-dollar bills to the slick-haired, fox-faced Mafioso behind the counter and asked for Bolivars, expecting about three hundred. The Mafioso gave me a blank stare for a second. His eyes narrowed, his eyebrows merged to one, and his lip curled in disdain.

"Do you wish bol eev' reys, *senõr?*" The olive oil in his tone did not mask his contempt.

I nodded. Five minutes in Venezuela, and already I was an ugly American. My tutor whipped out a pad of thousand-bol eev' rey notes and counted out 25 of them, but he wasn't done. Next came eight 500s, three 100s and two 20s. He counted the pile out to me like any kindergarten teacher would to a retarded student. The total was 29,340 bol eev'reys for 60 bucks. So much for my trusty dictionary.

The pile of bills was too big for a pocket. I rolled them up and stuck them in a suitcase. A pair of glass doors led outside into sunshine that cut through even my fog. The air smelled like pineapples, or maybe passion fruit. Definitely not like the tundra or the Kuskokwim. A line of taxis seemed to be sleeping along a circular drive.

Renaldo's instructions weren't needed. I just climbed into an ancient Pontiac with a taxi sign on top and said, "El Conde". The driver closed his copy of *Oui* magazine. It was in French, but I guess some things don't require translation. He put the magazine on the seat where his chauffeur's cap had been, adjusted the cap over salt-and-pepper hair, and checked me out in the rearview mirror.

Apparently I passed inspection because he said, "Si Señor," and we blasted out onto a highway as if we were riding in a Sherman tank. The highway was shelved into the side of a mountain. The scenery looked rugged, tropical and exciting, but the moment I sat down and stretched my legs in that warm cab, my eyes closed.

Horns and diesels woke me to the cacophony of the city. Caracas is a good-sized city, about four million people, I guess. It wasn't the steaming tropical cauldron I had expected at ten degrees above the equator, because it's around three thousand feet above sea level. It had the usual urban high-rises, but they seemed jumbled; all mixed together with different-sized buildings and set at different angles.

Most of the buildings we passed had fancy facades, as if each had been designed by an artist bent on personal expression. Plumeria, mango, banana, and a lot of trees I didn't recognize, gave the city a comfortable small-town feeling. I did see a pair of familiar golden arches on top of a building, so we wouldn't starve. The tip off to the city's size was air pollution. On top the hills the air quality was about like Seattle or Anchorage, but the valleys ranked with Mexico City or LA.

Parque Centrale went by, green trees and grass through a blue haze, just enough vegetation to provide a haven for muggers. The taxi screeched into the loading zone at the El Conde, and the driver announced that my fare was 13,300 bol eev'reys. I gave him two U.S. bills, a twenty and a ten. He smiled like Christmas morning, but let me unload my own bags.

The Conde was a mid-sized old-timer but recently remodeled. The bell captain was ageless, with coal black hair slicked back to reveal a high smooth forehead, but his eyes were ancient. Maybe he'd seen it all. He wore a sharp blue uniform with enough gold braid for a navy admiral or an usher at Lowe's Midland. He spoke excellent English, that wasn't the problem.

"Smith," I said.

"We have several, *señor.*"

"John Smith."

"*Si, señor,* still several."

"Mustache, like a pair of steer horns, jet black." I used my hands to pantomime the handlebars on a bicycle.

"*Si señor, uno momento, por favor.*" He picked up his phone and dialed.

"*Señor* Smith will meet you in the bar." He smiled. I tipped him two dollars, and he smiled again, so it must have been enough. I left my suitcases, and he was still smiling. I was getting the drift that a U.S. dollar was worth about 500 bolivars, but who knew what a bolivar was worth? I wandered through the lobby, enchanted by the colorful tiles on floor and walls, and into the spacious, wood-paneled bar.

It wasn't a New York bar, but it could have been in Miami or LA. Not that the bar itself was so different, but the patrons scattered around were relaxed and unfocused. No one was networking. It looked like maybe they just stopped in for a drink.

Renaldo came bouncing in with springs on his heels, looking like an *Esquire* model for tropical suits. He took charge of the bar like the star of a quiz show entering the stage. Energy and bonhomie radiated out from him. He spread his arms wide to envelop the whole bar, maybe the whole world, and waited until everyone responded before he zeroed in on me. I saw the advantage of his mustache. It added six inches to his smile.

I had ordered a rum and Coke when the bartender had come over to my table. I asked for Captain Morgan and settled for dark Meyers, all very quiet, but Renaldo shouted clear across the bar.

"Hey, Benny, would you make me one of those Hurricanes you learned to do so well in New Orleans?"

Benny beamed, of course, and started mixing. I marveled again at how the heck Renaldo did it. He'd been here maybe two days, three at the most, and already he knew the bartender, and no doubt the bellmen, by name, including their life histories. The women on the staff would be "Honey" or "Dear", and the funny thing was that he meant it, in his way, and they knew it and responded to him.

We didn't waste any time on "How you been?" or "Good to see you." When Renaldo and I sit down together, whether it's been a year or five, we just take up where we left off. It didn't matter that we were in a bar in Caracas. It could have been the sheep ranch in Australia, or the dive in Singapore, or even that tent on a glacier in Greenland; we were still just two boys sitting in front of the window in our dorm room.

I could see how Renaldo had been, and it was pretty good for a guy who was dodging bullets. He'd had more sun. He was bronzing like an ad for a tanning lotion. Perpetual smile lines were beginning to etch into his face. In college he might have been pretty, but now he was becoming ruggedly handsome. He didn't need the handlebar mustache anymore. People would turn around to look at him anyway.

"We've got to get back to the mine this evening," he said.

"I thought people there were shooting at you."

"Yeah, that's why we've got to get back."

We downed our drinks, Renaldo swung by the dispensary to give Benny a high-five and drop a bill on the bar. He had brought his suitcase down, so he discussed Conchita's operation with the bellman while I collected my bags, and a lot boy produced Renaldo's car.

We threw our bags, my two cloth-covered cardboard and his leather Gucci, into the trunk of his Jaguar. It was the SV8 hardtop that seems a little feminine until you feel the surge of power.

Renaldo threaded us out through the traffic, just the way you like to see a pilot fly. He was thinking a block or more ahead, so everything he did had already been planned. We passed a lot of government buildings, Nacional this, and Bolivar that. Pretty soon we were on the Avenue Sucre, and the city was petering out like Queen's Boulevard passing Kew Gardens.

The Avenue Cota Mil took us out of the city to a residential sprawl. I was surprised to see people walking along the freeway. A bunch of students scurried across an off ramp like a herd of migrating caribou crossing Steese Highway in Alaska. They survived and trotted on down the freeway, so we sure as heck weren't in California. We merged onto the Autopista Caracas - La Guaira. I had to hand it to those Venezuelans, naming Autopistas for the places they went rather than for dead presidents.

"Want to tell me about the shooting?" I asked.

"Shootings," he said, emphasizing the plural. "Two of my partners and Consuela. It's getting as bad as Washington, D.C."

"Can you get any more specific?"

"Well, there are always a lot of guns around. When you get into the hills, everyone you meet is either Wild Bill Hickok or Pancho Villa. We keep armed guards around the perimeter of the mine, about like the average SAC Base during the cold war. They shoot trespassers now and then. There's a corridor around the mine that's posted, 'Trespassers will be SHOT,' and they are. We have to do that to protect the gold."

"Is that legal?" I asked.

"Yep. This isn't the United States, you know. Private property is sacred here, and you have a right to protect it, unless the government decides to nationalize you. So far that's only happened to the oil companies."

We climbed and curved through low mountains that could have been the Appalachians or the Poconos except that the trees were mangos, eucalyptus, tangan- tangan, and a lot I didn't recognize. Shantytown, cardboard and roofing tin dwellings, were scattered through the trees beside the highway for several miles.

There were pines. I don't think there's any place with trees that doesn't have pines, but there were some pretty strange trees, too. The mountains got higher and rougher. We crossed bridges that made me cringe, and blasted through a tunnel.

When the next tunnel came up, Renaldo stomped the throttle and popped on the headlights. That tunnel must have been a couple of miles long, and before we got through it, we were both gasping for breath. We're spoiled in the U.S. where tunnels have lights and air is pumped through them. You might not believe the part about the air if you've ever been stalled in the Lincoln Tunnel during rush hour, but it's there.

These tunnels were just holes through the mountains. After the third tunnel, each time we climbed a hill it was lower than the last, smaller rocks, more trees, and pretty soon we started getting glimpses of the Caribbean.

"I assume your partners and Consuela were not trespassing," I prompted him.

"No, I'm just trying to set the scene. These were more

like executions in Brooklyn or Watts. Zeke was shot when he answered his doorbell."

"Zeke?" I asked.

"Ezekiel Gomez. Everyone here is named from the Bible. Everyone is Catholic, so most are named Joseph or Jesus but some people try to be different."

"I see," I said, "so Zeke answered his door. What about Joseph?"

"Jose' was driving home from the mine and someone shot him through the car window. He had bulletproof windows, but the air conditioner was broken so he had the window down."

"And Consuela?"

"She was sitting in my living room reading a newspaper, and someone shot her through the window."

"Thinking she was you?"

"Well, she was sitting in my chair, and she was reading the *Economica Hoy*. That's the newspaper from Caracas, and she was holding it up in front of her face."

We did a roller coaster leap onto the last mountain and started a series of hairpin turns down toward the ocean. Renaldo whipped us through the curves like a kid in a video arcade who has mastered the racecar simulator. The tires howled, but otherwise the Jag didn't mind.

"What's different? What's changed lately?"

"Nothing much. We hit a particularly rich vein a couple of weeks ago, so the gold shipments have been larger, but otherwise it's business as usual."

"Tell me about the business," I suggested.

"I really don't know a heck of a lot about the mining. I handle the books, shipping, payroll, all of that. I tell you,

Alex, gold mining is unbelievably profitable. We're making money faster than the U.S. Mint."

It turned out we weren't headed to the mine. We wheeled into La Guaira on the coast, arced around a business district and started uphill again. We passed a park, trees, grass, and flowers on the right, downhill side, and a theater with a lighted marquee on the left. Then mansions with walled courtyards were on both sides, with the business district one block away toward the ocean.

For a second I thought the lights on the left side were in the biggest building I'd ever seen, a thousand feet high and a couple of miles long, but it was individual houses crammed together on a hillside so steep they appeared to be stacked. We turned left and climbed one block up the hill, looking down on the mansions, and came into a tier of houses that looked as if they belonged to professionals, doctors who haven't been sued yet or lawyers who haven't been indicted.

We turned left again, back the way we came, but a hundred feet higher. Renaldo's place was the third on the uphill side; the downhill side was a hundred-foot drop into courtyards. He parked the Jag in a car-length driveway that stuck up into his property on a 45-degree angle. He opened the trunk, the suitcases tumbled out, and we caught them. He led the way up a half dozen stone steps to a three-foot wide lawn terrace and a verandah. I noticed I was looking up underneath the house on the street above us.

The verandah led past a big picture window to a front entrance. Renaldo opened the door and snapped on the light in a carpeted living room. The room, like the front lawn, was long but thin. I could see why. The front of the house was on fill, and the back, twenty feet toward the mountain, was actually dug into the hillside. If the house had been any deeper, it would have been underneath the house on the street above us. I learned later that there wasn't any street above us because there wasn't room. The next tier had only a dirt path.

We set our bags on the beige carpet, and Renaldo went to mix some drinks. I walked over and looked out through the big picture window we had just passed on the verandah. The view directly in front was across the street and down into courtyards. The courtyards surrounded mansions, or maybe haciendas. The grounds looked like mosaic tiles, blue pools and green shrubbery. Beyond the conspicuous affluence, a respectable city skyline spiked upward. Off to the right I could see a glimpse of the park we'd passed, silhouetted against a slice of the Caribbean. The view was spoiled by a bullet hole the size of a quarter in the middle of the glass.

Renaldo didn't have to ask; he brought me a rum and Coke, and I knew it was Captain Morgan as soon as the vanilla and spices passed under my nose. Either Venezuela is a civilized country after all, or Renaldo had imported civilization to it. It's not that I'm a one-drink man. In Alaska, when the last plane is tied down for the night, I pour a third of a cup of Bailey's Irish Cream into my coffee, and some situations call for Black Russians, which can be just as warming.

If I'm in San Francisco's Ghiradelli Square, I just naturally want an Irish Coffee, and in Miami I might even drink a piña colada, but when I need orienting, my body wants Captain Morgan and Coke.

"What did the shot sound like?" I asked.

"I didn't hear a shot. I was in the kitchen and I heard a 'tink' which must have been the glass breaking. When I came back in here Consuela had the paper laying against her face, like she might have gone to sleep. Then I saw there was a hole in the paper and blood was soaking through it."

"What kind of car?"

"There wasn't any car. I switched off the light and ran to the window and didn't see anyone at all."

"That's funny." I switched off the light and we looked out the window together. It wasn't dark outside yet but the sun was gone behind the hills. "If he wasn't on the porch he'd have had to be ten feet tall; and if he wasn't on the lawn, he'd have had to be twenty feet tall." I switched the light back on. We sipped some more. Renaldo's drink was clear, gin and tonic for him.

"Where's the chair?" I asked.

"It's in the spare bedroom. I cleaned it up, but I don't want to see it."

"Let's bring it out." We set our drinks on a coffee table and Renaldo led the way. The house had a kitchen on the left end of the living room and a stairway and hall behind the living room. The hall led to two bedrooms and a bath on the right. The bedroom at the back was under the stairway and didn't have any windows because it was against the hillside. It was a good place to store disfavored furniture.

The chair was a black leather Barcalounger, and it took both of us to carry it. It had a hole in the headrest and the stuffing was ripped out behind the hole. When we looked, we could see the indentations in the carpet that the chair legs had made. We set the chair exactly in the original spot.

"Was she leaning back?" I asked.

"About one notch. Comfortable, but not reclining."

I sat down in the chair and clicked it back. I felt for

the bullet hole with the back of my head and looked out through the hole in the window. I was looking up at a pretty good angle, and the shot looked impossible until I focused on what I could see. A block away, just past the mansions that were below my line of sight anyhow, loomed a high-rise with about a hundred windows looking our way.

"Hey," I said, "she wasn't shot with a pistol."

"I never said she was. Somebody said something about a 300 Savage."

I felt pretty stupid, but it had been a long day. In Alaska, we use rifles for moose and caribou. People and bears usually get shot with pistols, and I just assumed...well, I know better, of course. Foreign country, different customs.

"What's in that building?" I asked.

"Offices, mostly. Dentists, lawyers, real estate, insurance, stuff like that."

My line of sight through the bullet hole was approximately the tenth floor, and just a little left of center on the building. A few windows were lighted, most were dark.

Steps clicked across the porch, and I knew it was a woman before she passed the window. She was wearing high heels, and for a man to make that much noise he'd have to weigh five hundred pounds. I got a glimpse of gold and a cloud of black hair streaming behind her.

She charged straight in the door and grabbed Renaldo. She was almost Renaldo's height, at least in the spike heels, and she had the figure you might call *beanpole*. She was covered from neck to heels in a golden gown. The term *brocade* came to mind, but I'm not sure if they make gowns out of that, or only drapes. Anyhow it had a tight little collar that struck me as Chinese and long sleeves that fit her arms like gloves. Let me tell you, beanpoles can be very feminine and sexy. The cloud of black satin hair settled down and reached below her waist. The way she was kissing Renaldo, I wondered if I should excuse myself for a while.

They came up for air, so I tried to make that throat-clearing sound that works in movies. "I take it this is not Consuela?"

"No." He turned her around to stand beside him, but they still had arms around each other. She had that noble, slender face that's shared by Indians and Israelites. It can be fearsome on an Indian warrior, but *striking* was the word for her.

"Maria, this is my amigo Alex from Alaska. Alex, Maria is the cook."

Well, if the men were named Joseph and Jesus, then the women should be named Maria. "And Consuela was. . .?"

"My housekeeper."

I guess that explained quite a lot. I just had some more cultural adjustments to make.

Maria peeled loose and glided into the kitchen. That building looming with a view into the room from fifty windows gave me the creeps. I asked Renaldo to fetch a sheet, and together we hung it over the window.

Chapter 3

Maria cooked like James Beard. She spread a white cloth over a table in the back corner of the living room and laid out plates, silver, napkins, china cups and crystal wine glasses like a fancy restaurant. I almost expected candles, and wondered if I should put on a necktie. A rare rack of lamb béarnaise, with those little red potatoes and spears off a giant broccoli, was served up with Pinot Noir. Maria joined us and stuffed in about as much lamb and potatoes as Renaldo and I put together. I don't know where she put it because I could have circled her waist with my hands.

"Wonderful fresh vegetables you have here." I was really impressed by the broccoli.

"They should be. They're flown in fresh from California every day. The lamb is from New Zealand, and has never been frozen." That from Renaldo, Maria's mouth was full.

Renaldo and I talked a steady stream, but not catching up on recent events. We talked about things we both knew, like college, and some about Renaldo's cattle ranch in Oklahoma before the foot and mouth disease. He asked about the bar he'd bought in Anchorage just after the Russian Mafia set up their protection racket. I assured him that Gustave had rebuilt the bar in spite of the National Guard's blowing it to bits. We did some "I wonder what happened to so-and-so," but neither of us seemed to know.

Maria brought coffee, but suddenly my day caught up with me and my eyes closed. Renaldo jumped up and grabbed my bags. I managed to follow him up the staircase, long and narrow again. He set my bags inside a room at the front of the house, but all I saw was a queen-sized bed.

It had been a long day, in more ways than one. I'd flown around villages all day and then from Bethel to Anchorage on Wien Airlines, to Seattle on Alaska Airlines, to Atlanta to Miami on Eastern, and finally to Maiquetia. Each stop was just long enough to stretch my legs, usually at a dead run between gates, but not to rest. By the time I boarded the Servivensa flight in Miami, I was a zombie. I know, that's two days; but if you never stop, it seems like one.

When I woke up, it was daylight. I had no idea what day it was, but I couldn't think why it should matter. I found a bathroom down the hall and then went back and unpacked my bags. The closet had hangers and an empty dresser had more drawers than there are in my whole cabin. I snapped the pistol back together and loaded it but stuck it in the drawer with my socks.

Downstairs a note was propped on the table beside a coffee cup. "Good morning, Rip Van, I'm at work, home around three, coffee in kitchen, food in fridge. Renaldo." Apparently Maria didn't cook breakfast. I melted some butter in a frying pan, tossed in a chunk of leftover lamb, and scrambled some eggs beside it.

I left the pistol in the drawer and set out to explore. The air was soft, heavy, and warm like a cotton blanket. It smelled of a nice mixture of ocean and flowers like L.A. used to smell about ten million cars ago. I turned left and walked in the street because there wasn't any sidewalk. The right-hand side was a straight drop into lawns and swimming pools behind the mansions below me.

At the corner, I turned left again and started up the hill. When I get into a new town, I need to check it out. I'm not comfortable until I get a sense of where I am. I think the reason that men are always vilified for not wanting to ask directions is that when a guy gets into a new town he wants to learn the layout. In fact, he's probably more interested in learning the area than he is in getting to Aunt Minnie's house.

The road leveled out for a few feet to make a landing between rows of houses. It wasn't a street between the houses, just a dirt path, and the road I was on got steeper, if possible. The road ended between another couple of tiers of dwellings and the houses were noticeably smaller and had even less paint than the ones below. Between the tiers was a dirt alley with roofs on the left side and braces to hold houses up on the right. I turned around and had a magnificent view, over the city and out across the water. Hills curved out toward the ocean on both ends of town, wild, green, jungle covered. Wooden steps replaced the road and continued up. Might as well start at the very top and work back.

The stairs ended, and so did the houses, but there was still a trail going up. I stood on the landing at the top of the stairs and did a full circle. It was glorious. The world still had a morning feel to it, but the sun was a lot higher than it ever gets in Alaska. It looked on track to pass directly overhead, and it seemed to have a personal interest in making Venezuela comfortable.

The town below looked small and clean. The business district ran right down to docks on the far side. I could see a hundred miles of Caribbean. A couple of cruise ships were white toys on the ocean, and some small islands on the right were emeralds. The breeze had picked up and had a freshness to it like the arctic, only warm. I was higher than some of the other hills, so I could see that valleys ran parallel to the ocean like a giant plowed field.

The trail that continued up was just a dirt path, but well traveled and worn a foot deep through some carpeting plant like heather. I could see more dwellings up the trail, but they couldn't be called houses. They were shacks, plywood and roofing tin nailed together and leaning against the mountain. This I had to see. It seemed to me that La Guaira was upside down by North American customs. We always have the slums at the bottom and the mansions on top. I climbed on up the trail.

A few side trails led to shacks, or hovels. The main trail curved around to the left and leveled somewhat. Brush and trees crowded the trail from the uphill side. The trail turned into a shelf, clinging to the steep side of the mountain. I came around a little scallop in the hill and saw that the trail ran straight into a dwelling and ended. The dwelling couldn't be called a shack, or even a hovel. It was several sheets of corrugated steel roofing propped against the side of the mountain, and that was it. I could see the trail widen out to make a dirt floor under the roofing.

Reality kicked in and I felt very much a trespasser. With no more branches from the trail, I was in someone's private entry, and it was pretty obvious that I had come to gawk, and not exactly in admiration. I stopped and would have turned around, but a young woman, early twenties I think, came out of that cave. I stood and stared.

She was a pretty girl, heart-shaped face with the high cheekbones you see in magazine ads for cosmetics. Her black, shoulder-length hair was brushed to a high sheen, and she was wearing just enough make up, but the thing that had me staring was her costume: heels and hose, pleated skirt and ruffled blouse. The blouse was pink, but the shoes and the skirt were spotless, shining, immaculate white, matched by a string of faux pearls. She came out of that hole in the ground looking cleaner than I had probably ever looked in my life.

I wish I could say she struck me like a minor chord in the Hallelujah Chorus, or a pastel touch up in a Ruben's painting. What came to mind was a song from Sesame Street. *One of these things is not like the others, one of these things just doesn't belong...* They show an apple, an orange, a banana, and a kangaroo. Little Susie or Johnny is supposed to pick out the misfit. That young woman would have fit if she had stepped out of a castle in a Disney movie.

There wasn't room to pass on the trail. I scrambled up the hill and held onto a bush so she could get by me. She gave me a friendly open smile as if we were meeting on a city street instead of me invading her territory. I stood there, dumbstruck, for a decent interval, and then followed her down.

I stayed a block behind her, but close enough to admire her queenly, confident posture: head high, proud chest, and precise graceful steps in the high heels. The view receded, the breeze lessened, it got hotter and more humid. We passed better and better houses in worse and worse locations until finally we were between the courtyards of the super rich. They had no breeze at all, and a view limited to the inside of their courtyards.

Our street was level for the final block and ended at an intersection with the perimeter of the commercial district. Department stores and shops weren't Fifth Avenue, but they could have been Des Moines. My lovely little dove from the mountain blended with the shoppers and ducked into a department store. Two ships had passed in the night.

The building I had eyed through Renaldo's bullet hole was a block down the street to my right. The sidewalk was crowded, people milling in and out of music stores, beauty parlors, a *joyeria*. That sign caught my imagination, but it apparently meant jewelry store. Most buildings were two-and-three-story with businesses on the first floor and what appeared to be apartments above them. The monolith I was looking for had an awning over the sidewalk and a continuation of the shops, but it went up, way up, stark and unadorned like a domino standing on end.

A couple of marble steps led to pretentious etched glass double doors, but the pretense stopped at the doorway. The tiles on the floor in the lobby showed a well-worn path to the elevators. Those ancient cages had dials above them, like a one-handed clock to indicate which floor the car was on.

The clock showed a couple of Bs for basement, then a G, which is what the elevator registered when it stopped. The next floor up was labeled "1", European style instead of "2," the way it would have been in the United States. I guess neither way is more correct, or less confusing. Maybe it's just a need to be different. "If you drive on the left, then by golly, I'll drive on the right."

I punched an U*p* button and climbed into the first cage that opened. The outside door slid shut and then a metal cage door closed. People who have toddlers, or other pets, sometimes put blockades like that in their doorways. Those are usually made of wooden dowels that spread like an accordion to fill the space. The grate on the elevator was flat steel bars, but the effect was the same. The walls of the shaft going by and the doors that passed were visible. I punched *ten* and watched the floors go by.

A floor directory across the hall from the elevator confirmed Renaldo's list of tenants. Ten seemed to be the insurance floor, and several of the offices were vacant. I walked along the hall, checking doors on the uphill side. At the end of the hallway, I took the stairs down to the ninth floor and inspected doors back to the other end. A mirror image staircase led up to the eleventh and I started down the hall on eleven. Most of that floor was vacant except for one office right across from the elevators. The stencil on the door was *Especialista en Endodontura,* but the emanations seeping into the hall were the unmistakable aromas of a dentist's office. Two doors past the dentist's office, I found what I was looking for. The old wooden doorframe had dents where someone had pried against the wood around the latch. The long blade of my penknife slipped behind the molding next to the latch, and the door swung open.

The first room had apparently been a reception area, desk and chair on the right, broken and sagging couch on the left, with an empty magazine rack beside it. The place was clean except for a layer of dust indicating it had been vacant for a while. The floor was a pattern of white nine-inch asphalt tiles, set on the bias to make diamond shapes, with black tiles every four feet to accent the pattern. Footprints in the dust led straight across the room. A dark narrow hallway went both ways, with one set of footprints going right and coming back, and several sets going left. I took the road more traveled.

Sherlock Holmes or Hercule Poirot might have learned quite a lot from those footprints. What I learned was that it was either a man, or a woman wearing low heels, and they weren't very tall because at 5'10" I was easily out-striding them. I decided to deduce that they had black hair. In Venezuela that gave me better than a ninety-nine percent chance of being right.

The hallway ended with a door that stood open into an empty room with windows looking up at the hills. The windows were the old-fashioned wooden sashes with two panes that slid up or down. One sash near the center had been raised and left a couple of inches open. I studied the hillside for a minute, easily picking out Renaldo's house, and even noted a rusty gleam from the aerie where I had flushed the classy little dove.

The shooter had knelt on the floor to do the deed, and from the marks I deduced that he or she was wearing pants that had dust on the knees until it was brushed off. The shot had been good, but not remarkable, assuming a telescopic sight, and assuming the 300 Savage rumor was correct.

Memory said the original 300 Savage had a 24-inch barrel and spit out a 110-grain bullet at about 3,000 feet per second. Remington made some other models that used the same bullet, including a semi-automatic; but in any case we're talking high powered rifle, right up there with the .30-06, and a nearly flat trajectory from here to Renaldo's.

I looked around, but I didn't find any empty cartridges or any business cards fortuitously dropped at the scene. What I did determine, on very careful, Poirot-like investigation, although without a magnifying glass, was that the footprints were made at different times. Some had a little dust over them, but at least one set looked as fresh as mine. I checked again to be sure the sheet was still covering Renaldo's window.

The elevator creaked and swayed back to the lobby, and on a whim I walked back to the department store where my passing ship had disappeared. Except for signs in Spanish, it could have been any five-and-dime in Duluth or Anchorage. Renaldo's note had said "three." My watch said nine-twenty, but I hadn't bothered to count the time zones during my marathon flight.

I wandered through the store pretending to absorb culture and look for a clock until I spotted her, same regal head, proud chest, and pink blouse with faux pearls. She was reigning behind a costume jewelry counter. Highlights in her hair reflected and refracted the display lights as brightly as the items on her counter. She wore a tiny gold watch that was just the excuse for a guy with my savoir faire. I strolled casually up to her counter and used my entire Spanish vocabulary on her.

"*Por favor, que hora es?*" I asked.

When I got close, her perfume knocked my socks off. I wouldn't know what it was, but it put me in mind of diamonds and yachts and new Gulf Stream jets. She gave me the same friendly smile I had seen on the mountain, but I was pretty sure she didn't recognize me.

"*Son las dos y veinte,*" she said. Her voice made me wonder if leopards purr.

I smiled my *gracias*, and gathered enough wits to make a hasty retreat to neutral territory before I stopped to wrack my brain for translation. Twenty after two. I went out to check a few more streets, just to see where they went, before I climbed up to Renaldo's. I floated back past the domino building on a cloud of remembered perfume, trying to see something other than those haunting dark eyes.

The street past the domino building was the exit from an underground garage. Then came a block of single-family dwellings from the eighteen hundreds, or maybe older, but sharp and clean as if they'd been built, or at least painted, yesterday. I turned left one block and came to the waterfront. A boulevard ran next to the water with a low cement railing. The harbor was naturally enclosed by headlands and was at least a mile across. Sun glittered off a gentle chop on green water that looked deep.

Wooden docks ran a hundred feet out from the sidewalk. The fleet looked like work boats, rugged and practical with a homemade appearance about them. What was conspicuously absent was the sleek fiberglass pleasure boats that dominate North American marinas. I wound back through a brick-and-stone canyon that again evoked a previous century, and climbed the hill to Renaldo's domain.

Chapter 4

I beat Renaldo home, and by the time he got there I had taken down the sheet from the window and was working with clothes hangers to make my old purple bathrobe sit up straight in the Barcalounger. Renaldo came in wearing a light tan tropical suit with a red tie and a gold nugget tack. Some guys are just born to wear suits, and he was one. He made the suit look sharp and comfortable at the same time.

He headed straight for the kitchen and came back carrying a rum and Coke and a gin and tonic before he stopped to ask what the heck I was doing.

"I'm making a shooting gallery," I explained. "This is the wooden duck. Are you any good at drawing?"

"Top of my class in kindergarten. Whatcha want drawn?"

"Wad up some newspapers the size of a small pumpkin, wrap them in a dish towel and draw a face on it like a jack-o-lantern."

All that Glisters // 39

"Can do. You want the traditional triangle nose and a couple of missing teeth?"

"No, let's make it really scary. Give it pencil-line designer eyebrows, a minimal nose, and draw the mouth shut, but put a ridiculous gigantic black mustache on it."

He apparently got the idea, because by the time I got the book to stand up in my mannequin's hands, he came back with a head that was recognizable. He had done better than a dishtowel. He'd found a big cloth napkin that was the right shade of tan and used a black magic marker to draw his face and hair on it. He stood and sipped juniper juice while I perched the head on top the clothes hanger.

"What's he reading?" Renaldo wondered.

"It's a 1967 almanac. You really should update your library." We stood there, admiring our handiwork and sipping courage.

"Is Maria coming back tonight?" I asked.

"If a clock says six, she'll be here. Angelus shall ring tonight."

"Can you give her a call and stop her?"

"No phone, but I guess I could nip up the hill and give her the night off."

"She lives in that warren above us?"

"About halfway up. I pay her 12,500 bolivars a week for cooking and it moved her two tiers down the hill."

"Renaldo, say just hypothetically, that a very pretty girl was working a counter in a department store. How much would she earn in a week?"

"Maybe nine, ten thousand. There are plenty of good jobs here. Venezuela is a manufacturing economy and a rich one, but you have to have papers. If you're working a counter, there's something wrong with your papers. Maybe you crossed a border without noticing it, or maybe your great granddaddy took a shot at Bolivar or stole a horse. If you don't have papers, you take what you can get. There are six people lined up for every service job, so they don't have to pay, and they don't. A lot of people in this town would be happy to work sixty hours for an American ten-dollar bill."

"I gather the exchange rate is about 490 bolivars to the dollar?"

"It's 495, but that's this week. Don't count on it."

"Has it gone up since yesterday?"

"No, it's been stable for months. Why?"

"I think I got ripped off at the airport yesterday, I got less than 490." I'm not smart enough to figure that out in my head. Maybe it's a pilot thing, but I expect other people use the technique too. I've heard it called *guesstimating*. A lot of times you don't need an exact figure, but you need a quick answer.

When the guy at the airport gave me 29,340 bolivars for 60 bucks, I automatically figured that nine times six is 54, so less than 29,400 is less than 490, but not much less. That's close enough for government work, or deciding whether you have enough fuel to make a particular destination. You're not looking to split hairs, you want a resounding yes or no and you want it fast.

Renaldo cleared up the mystery. "You exchanged money at Ital Cambio and got 489. It's called a commission, but it's considered a rip off for gringo suckers. What we do here is round everything up to the nearest 500, figure 500 bolivars to the dollar, and pay in American money. It's close enough and anyone who's cheap enough to count parts of a penny will know they're getting a good deal."

We'd finished our drinks and it wasn't the right time to start more.

"Is anyone really that cheap?" I wondered.

"You'd be amazed. Most people here are either rolling in dough or one step ahead of starvation. If you're on the bottom of the heap, a few bolivars can mean the difference between surviving and not."

For some reason that made me a little sick to my stomach, but then I remembered that the last time I was in San Francisco I was stepping over panhandlers in the business district. I had come out of a cafe on Van Ness Avenue and met a nice-looking woman in her forties with two teenage kids. The boy was about fifteen, the girl maybe thirteen, and all three of them were clean and neatly dressed. The woman stopped me and explained that the soup kitchen they had come to for supper was closed. Could I help them out with money for food?

The only cash I had with me was a ten-dollar bill and I gave her that. Afterward, when it was too late, I wished I'd taken them to a restaurant for dinner. Problem is, you can't save the world. Anyhow, I hadn't seen any panhandlers in Venezuela, and no gray-haired ladies with paper bags stacked around them, ready to defend a heat vent with their lives the way they do in New York.

"Shall we take a walk?" I asked.

Renaldo changed to loafers, chinos, and a short-sleeved shirt, and we wandered back up the road I had taken in the morning. We turned left at the bottom of the stairs and walked along a path between the roofs of houses on our left and stilts under houses on our right. We had a nice breeze and a view of half the coast of Venezuela. Renaldo picked a house on the right, and we climbed up an affair that was half stairs and half ladder.

We only got as far as the porch. Four people were sitting on chairs on the long narrow verandah. A couple of kids were playing on the floor. A little girl was setting up a row of dolls, and a little boy was mowing them down with a stick that was an imaginary machine gun, helping them out with his foot when they didn't fall satisfactorily. The machine gun was pretty loud, a Chinese SKS, I think. It made a "tat-tat-tat" sound that required the full capability of a lusty pair of four-year-old lungs.

Maria dropped what looked like knitting and ran to give Renaldo his hug and kisses. One of the handsomest young Latins I've ever seen was right behind her, giving Renaldo a hug, and I thought for a minute he was going to kiss Renaldo too.

"Alex," Renaldo said, "you met Maria last night. This is her husband Juan, her parents, and Juan and Maria Jr. are over there operating the firing squad."

Juan rushed to shake my hand, gripping my elbow with his other hand to make it doubly sincere. Juan wasn't very tall, a couple of inches shorter than Maria, but he was thick and solid. The way he walked and the way he filled his clothes put me in mind of a Clydesdale. When he smiled, it was apparent that all toothpaste commercials should be made in Venezuela. I nodded solemnly to each of Maria's parents. Strike that last statement. They had no teeth at all.

Renaldo explained the situation to Maria and Juan, I think. Anyway, he told them something in rapid Spanish and they nodded. Maria continued to hang on Renaldo's arm while he went over and handed each of the kids a tightly rolled bill. The kids took the bills and stuffed them into pockets, but continued the carnage. That's the closest I've ever seen Renaldo come to being ignored. I thought for a second he was going to dig out more bills and try again, but he settled for patting heads, and more or less carried Maria back to the stairs.

I sneaked a glance at Juan to see how he was taking Maria's manhandling, or womanhandling, of Renaldo. What I saw was pure adoration. Juan was as proud of Maria as if he'd made her himself, and so confident in his own masculinity that jealousy would never occur to him.

We seemed to be leaving. Juan rushed to pump my hand again. I looked straight into those frank, honest brown eyes, and I could see all the way to his soul. He was a sweet little boy who wanted very much to please. We did the usual awkward waving and nodding, and climbed down the stairs backward.

"Good heavens," I blurted, "surely that Juan could get a job?"

"Juan doesn't exist," Renaldo explained. "Juan used to be a foreman at a bauxite mine. A couple of characters hassled Maria, so Juan took a machete and made hamburgers out of them. When the *policia* showed up, Juan was still steaming, and he started on the cops. That was his mistake. They pulled his papers."

"So?" We turned down the hill. I wasn't getting it.

"Not so different from the U.S." Renaldo pointed out. "Suppose they deleted your social security number, what would you do?"

It took a minute before the ramifications started to gel. Pilot's license, driver's license, credit cards, checking account, apartment lease, any job at all. I began to get the picture.

"Couldn't he have papers forged?" I wondered.

"Could, but that's a hanging offense."

We climbed back up the stairs at Renaldo's, and he mixed us each one more drink. We rigged a floor lamp to light the dummy and unplugged it from the wall so that Renaldo could turn the light on without showing himself in the window. I went up to my room, shoved the pistol into my belt, and put on a dark blue windbreaker to cover it.

"Plug the lamp just before it gets dark," I said. I walked back down the hill, dragged myself past the store with the golden goddess at the jewelry counter, and shoved through the big glass doors into the domino building. The lobby was deserted, and it looked as if that was usually the case. I took the elevator up to the tenth floor. I didn't want an elevator sitting there with its pointer on eleven. When I got to ten it occurred to me that all I had to do was punch *G* when I stepped off, so I did that.

The stairs to the eleventh floor seemed to be amplified. I was trying to be quiet, but my steps, my hand sliding on the rail, even my breathing echoed up and down the stairwell. I shoved the door at the landing and peeked down the hallway. The block-long tunnel was deserted. White floor tiles, wooden doors on both sides, fluorescent fixtures lined the ceiling, some bright, some dark, some flickering. No lurkers were apparent. Lights were still on in the dentist's office, and a murmur of voices was just discernable. I crept to the door that had been jimmied and cursed myself for not being a detective in a novel. On my first visit I should have put a hair, or a thread, or something somewhere so I could tell if the door had been opened, but I hadn't thought of it. Then I wondered if the shooter had.

I stood beside the door with my nose against the wall and reached with my left hand to shove the knife blade past the latch, just in case someone decided to perforate the door. The door swung open, and nothing else happened. Gun in hand, I ducked low and rushed in. The place was empty except for the magazine stand that I'd forgotten until I whacked it with my shin.

It was getting dark, but some light came from the windows in the offices and leaked into the back hallway. I shoved the door closed and limped the path less traveled to the right. It was a mirror image of the room I'd checked out earlier. I opened one of the windows enough that I could stick my head out and see the open window in the next room. The window was just the way I'd left it. No rifle barrel sticking out. I leaned against the wall where I'd be behind the door if someone checked, and I could see Renaldo's window without moving. I stood there, waiting for it to get dark and thinking about the jewelry salesgirl. I wondered how many people she had hacked to hamburger with her machete.

She made an intriguing picture, flailing away with a three-foot blade, blood flying, but never a speck landing on her immaculate outfit. Just for fun, I pictured her skirt riding up a bit when she swung.

I'd waited about an hour when I heard the outer door open and footsteps whispered across the tiles. They stopped at the intersection in the hallway, waited several heart thumps, and then turned left toward the other room. Waiting motionless for an hour was not a problem for me. For one thing, when my body stops, my mind seems to speed up, and I rather enjoy that, but also it's an old moose-hunting technique. Since a moose travels twenty miles a day while he's just browsing, there's no point trying to follow him. You just get comfortable and wait until he comes to you.

We waited together, me and he or she in the next room, while the sun went behind the mountains. Renaldo plugged in his reading light and the dummy was spotlighted. I didn't have a telescopic sight, but the imposter looked pretty good. I heard the slightest scrape from next door. I tippy-toed to peek out my window. About three feet of gun barrel were sticking out of the window next door. That was no 300 Savage that I'd ever seen.

With gun in hand I quit breathing while I soft-shoed down the hall. The door to the next room was still open. A man was kneeling in the dust by the window sighting a rifle. I stepped through the door just as he fired.

"Freeze!" I shouted. Corny, I know, but that's what I wanted him to do. I wanted that rifle barrel to stay outside the window. I needn't have worried. He let go of the stock when he jumped up and the whole rifle went out the window. He spun around and found my pistol three inches from his face. He ducked back and hit the old window sash with his shoulders. It didn't make a crack, just a sigh, but the glass exploded, and the little brown guy with the long black hair pinwheeled backward out the window.

I dropped the pistol and grabbed him around the knees when they went by. He was all cooperation, scrabbling at the window casing with his hands, and together we got him back inside. I dumped him on the floor, picked up the pistol, and stepped back.

"Get up," I said.

Blank stare.

"On your feet." Nothing.

That was a problem. I didn't want to get within his reach because he just might be a South American version of Bruce Lee. He looked like a twelve-year-old sitting there. His skin was darker than I'd been seeing on the streets, his hair longer than the local fashion, and he stared with the wide-eyed innocence of a Boy Scout with his first copy of *Playboy*. Problem was he might require only an eye blink to fly through the air and kick me senseless, or grab me by one finger and toss me out the window. The surest way to find out would be to reach for him, and the best defense is to stay far enough back so there's time to shoot if anything surprising happens.

It wasn't that I minded shooting him. If you pull a gun on someone, you'd better be prepared to shoot. Otherwise there isn't much point, and if you're using the gun as an empty threat, you'll probably end up being the one who gets shot. Still, I'd rather not shoot if it can be avoided, and I really wanted to ask this one some questions.

He was sitting on the floor, vulnerable, legs spread, hands on the floor, looking perfectly helpless, and that's what worried me. I took out my knife and tossed it up. It arced down toward his head and his eyes flicked up at the knife. I kicked him in the solar plexus, jumped back, and got away with it.

The knife had skittered three feet away from him. I scooped it up, grabbed a handful of mane and pulled the guy up by the hair. He probably weighed 100 pounds or less. I stuck the gun in the back of my belt, jerked both the guy's arms up behind him and held them there with my left hand.

He wasn't struggling with me, he was struggling to get some air back into his lungs. With my right hand, I snapped the knife blade open, and held it against his throat. A little more lift on his arms and we marched right along to the door.

I slammed him against the wall and held him there while I opened the door. The hallway was empty, so I marched him down the hall and pushed the elevator button. We'd just stepped into the cage when someone shouted, "*Uno momento*." The dentist stuck his white-coated arm in to hold the door. The dentist was around sixty, a little overweight, graying at the temples. He had the smooth skin of a television anchor with his make up on, or a man who has never stepped outdoors in his life.

The dentist looked perfectly calm when he saw me standing there holding the little guy with the knife at his throat. He gave me a perfunctory nod, turned to face front and held the door. The woman who hurried to join us was around forty, nice-looking motherly type.

The dentist punched the lobby button, and he and his assistant stood there pointedly facing front while we rode down. The only movement they made was a surreptitious squeeze of each other's hands. I'd have bet a lot that they were married, but not to each other. When the door opened at the lobby, they walked straight out into the street and I was right behind them.

Renaldo was on the sidewalk with the Jag parked at the curb and the door open. I shoved the shooter face down on the back seat and knelt backward in the passenger seat to hold him there while Renaldo drove us back to the house.

We tied the sniper's hands behind him and his ankles together and plunked him down in the chair where he had a good view of the window. There were now two holes in the window, an inch apart, and two holes in the headrest. Renaldo's work of art was lying on the floor behind the chair with a bullet hole between its eyebrows.

Renaldo brought our drinks.

"Ask him some questions," I suggested.

Renaldo tried for a while in Spanish. The only reaction from the little guy was to lick his lips when he saw my rum and Coke.

"Aren't we supposed to put splinters under his fingernails, or pound his toes with a hammer?" I asked. "Why not ask him what he prefers?"

Renaldo tried some more Spanish, sentences getting shorter, and finally the little guy spit out a half dozen staccato sentences of his own.

"Well, there's part of the problem," Renaldo elucidated. "He's not speaking Spanish. Portuguese, I think. I believe he wants you to hurry up and shoot him. He has shot your friend, so now you must shoot him."

I bent over behind the chair and picked up the dummy head. I held it in the shooter's face, showed him the bullet hole, and made a deprecating gesture as if he was the dumbest human on the planet. His eyes popped open until the lashes were tangled with his eyebrows. I'd let him get a good whiff of my drink, and he licked his lips again.

"Got any rum besides the Captain Morgan?" I asked.

"I think there's a bottle of Bacardi at the back of the shelf."

"Mix him a drink, about fifty-fifty, and put a straw in it."

Renaldo came back with a big glass, almost as pale as his gin and tonic, with a soda straw sticking out of it. I took the drink, sat on the chair arm, and put the straw in the guy's mouth. The way the liquid disappeared up the straw reminded me of a '48 Buick Slush-o-matic I used to have. It went through gasoline like that.

When the straw made that gurgling sound, Renaldo took the empty glass and went to mix another. *Mix* may not be the right word, he mostly just filled the glass with rum. I inserted the tube again and the siphon started.

"This guy knows things we really need to find out. How the heck are we going to do it?"

"I think I know an expert. Juan spent some time in jail. He'll probably have some good ideas." Renaldo set his drink down and went out to fetch Juan. Both of the rum glasses, mine and the hostage's, were empty, so I set them on the coffee table and went to sit across the room in another chair. Just to keep things in perspective, I took the pistol out of my belt and toyed with it on my lap.

Renaldo came back with a very happy, excited Juan in tow. I was struck again with what a handsome specimen Juan was, neat and clean in short-sleeved shirt, muscles bulging below the sleeves. His happy smile showed all 32 perfect, pearl-white teeth. Renaldo sat on a chair beside me, and Juan knelt on the floor in front of our prisoner.

"Chink!" Another plug of glass spurted out of the window, and there sat our hostage with a hole in his forehead and a trickle of blood starting down his nose. Renaldo grabbed Juan and jerked him back; I killed the light switch. Renaldo was stuffing bills into Juan's hands. "*Vamoose!*" Renaldo shouted at Juan.

Renaldo and I were already climbing into the Jag. Renaldo didn't turn on the headlights, so it was pretty dark.

The tires howled backing out of the driveway and again turning down the hill, and there wasn't any space between the howls. La Guaira has streetlights, but about half the number we're used to. We ripped down the block without driving off the hundred-foot drop into a courtyard, and screeched around the corners to park in front of the domino building.

"Do you have a gun?" I asked.

"What? Do you think I'm a cretin?"

"Here, take mine. Shoot the first two or three people who come out." I shoved the .357 into his hands and ran down the block. It had occurred to me that I had seen a parking garage entrance to that building on the next street. Sure enough, I got there just in time to see a black sedan spurt out of an underground exit. I whistled, and the Jaguar's tires screamed. Renaldo didn't stop for me, but he kicked the door open when he passed, and I made it inside before the tires screamed again.

In seconds we were out of town headed back up the highway, and the sedan was ahead, fishtailing around the hairpins above us, flashing headlights at the mountain and the valley after every turn. Moonlight was showing us the drop-offs and rocks that were waiting, just in case.

Renaldo was doing his video arcade routine again, and the Jag was hugging the highway as if it were on rails. The lights above us disappeared over the top, and seconds later we topped the ridge ourselves. On the first straight stretch, I was amazed to see the speedometer touch 190 before I realized it was kilometers.

We burned three miles of highway in one minute before Renaldo slowed down.

"What's wrong?" I shouted. I didn't need to shout; it was perfectly quiet in the Jag, but a shout seemed appropriate.

"Shouldn't there be some headlights up there somewhere?" Renaldo asked.

He had a point there. We could see two or three miles of road dipping down and curving around, like a snake's back in the moonlight. It was remarkably clear of cars.

Renaldo screeched to a stop and backed around in a half circle. We started back, going only 80 Kph. Just before the brow of the hill, a dirt road led off to our right. Black rubber tracks on the highway showed where a car had made the turn too fast. We'd have seen that if we'd been traveling at a reasonable speed, like maybe 150 kilometers per hour.

Two hard-packed dirt tracks with grass between them and trees meeting overhead followed the crest of the hill. I got out and walked behind the car for an unrestricted view. That's another nice thing about the Jag; I could see right over the top of it. I carried the .357 in my hand with the hammer back. Renaldo turned on more headlights than I ever knew a passenger car carried, and we inched our way down the dirt path into the woods.

We'd gone less than a hundred yards when we found the broken branches and tracks in the loose dirt where the sedan had turned around. Renaldo spun the Jag, and I jumped in. We exploded back out of the woods, fishtailed across the pavement, and blasted back over the edge of the hill toward town. A dozen cars were calmly going about their business around the town and the waterfront below us.

"Now what?" I asked.

"We're going to have to cook our own supper. Maria won't be down tonight."

We drove slowly and sedately down the hill. Cars along the park were empty, or were disgorging patrons for the movie theater across the street. A few cars drove along the boulevard beside the harbor. Every one of them looked to me like a black sedan.

Chapter 5

"Renaldo," I said, "there has to be a reason. If it were Juan shooting at you I could understand it, but that doesn't seem to be the case here."

Renaldo had to stop and think about that. It hadn't occurred to him that anyone could object to his smooching Maria. Maybe he was right. Renaldo and Maria were just a couple of hot-blooded, demonstrative Latins who happened to like each other. Apparently their intentions were honorable, and I had to assume Juan knew that.

We had hung the sheet across the window again. Renaldo had stuck a frozen pizza in the oven, so Venezuela was on the cutting edge of civilization. We were sharing out the pizza, with Renaldo grabbing the extra anchovies and me sneaking most of the mushrooms. Without Maria there to formalize dinner, we hadn't bothered to switch to wine.

The police had shown up and carried out the body. A

lieutenant counted three holes in the window and three holes in the chair, and was glancing around, maybe looking for the third body. Renaldo showed him the dummy head. The cop nodded, satisfied, and they left with no further questions.

I was in my big brother mode, pontificating. "It seems to me the problem is business related, unless all of your partners were smooching Maria. Now we know we're dealing with multiple shooters. Not only was there a second marksman who shot the one we'd captured, but I had the impression of two or three guys in that sedan."

Renaldo was nodding and thinking. I could tell he was thinking because his gin and tonic was evaporating pretty fast. He addressed his glass.

"It doesn't make sense. People try to steal the gold and shoot the guards, but what do they have to gain by shooting the office staff? Our business doesn't hurt anybody or compete with anybody. We dig out the gold and ship bags to our wholesaler in Miami. He sells to his retail contacts around the country and sends us back the cash."

"Cash?" I wondered.

"It's an IRS thing. The less paper trails, the less taxes he has to pay." Renaldo abandoned his glass to talk to me. "You don't suppose it's the IRS doing the shooting?"

"In Miami, probably. Here, I doubt it. You're not cooking the books, one set for the partners and another set for stockholders?"

"There aren't any stockholders. Just us six partners, four now. My partners were all established businessmen and easily bankrolled the mine themselves. We didn't need to raise a lot of capital because the gold mine doesn't have a big overhead. It's not like a placer mine with dredges and things. Here a crew goes into the mountain with picks in the morning and brings out sacks of gold at night."

"How many miners?" I wondered.

"Fifty miners and fifty security guards. There's cooks and janitors, expediters, truck drivers, this and that. Altogether just over two hundred men on the payroll."

That sounded about like an American business. Twenty-five percent to do the work, and seventy-five percent to take care of them and supervise.

"How about the partners? Any jealousy, any power struggles?"

"Not these guys. For one thing they're all related, cousins or something. Julio is the CEO and what he says goes. I don't think there's ever been a harsh word between them."

"Julio doesn't sound very biblical," I mused.

"Wasn't Julius Caesar in the Bible? Seems like he should have been, right place at the right time."

"Oh, sure, I guess so... 'Give unto Caesar that which is Caesar's...' He must have been." We let it ride. We had more serious problems, like both of our bottles running low.

"Do you want to come into the office with me tomorrow and look at the books?"

"I'd a heck of a lot rather visit the mine."

"Sounds like a good idea. Can you believe I've never actually been to the mine myself?"

That wasn't hard to believe. Mines are notorious for having dirt around. The closest Renaldo normally came to dirt was whatever might be dished around the water cooler in a business office. We finished our bottles and called it a night. I had a little trouble with the stairway weaving.

All that Glisters // 57

Renaldo turned toward his room below mine, and I saw the side of the hallway give him a whack on the shoulder.

I did go into the office with Renaldo in the morning, but not to check the books. Mostly it was to meet Julio, and to get the feel of the place. Renaldo wheeled into a parking garage and stuck a card into a slot. The arm didn't rise until a guard in a booth looked us over and pressed a button. We drove into a cement cavern lit by naked bulbs hanging from a too-low ceiling, following the path of oil dripped from many cars. We passed several luxury automobiles and found a parking space next to a bank of elevators. An apparent drunk was sleeping in his convertible just outside the elevators, but he was sleeping with one eye open. He had a coat spread over something on the seat beside him. It could have been a banjo. Renaldo gave him a nod and he closed his other eye.

When the elevator stopped on the fifth floor, a janitor was leaning against the wall, so he was behind us when we stepped out. He had a little bucket on wheels with a mop in it, but he had his right hand in his pocket. The offices were plain, simple, adequate. They were on the fifth floor of a ten-story brick dinosaur that overlooked the waterfront. There weren't any signs, but the one-way glass on the door was stenciled, *Mineral Corporacion*.

The offices reminded me of what I'd read about the Wal-Mart company. No showy headquarters, no ostentation, no glitzy public image. Wal-Mart brought more to the bottom line than any other company, and that's the way the headquarters struck me. Just a bare room with four unoccupied desks, and two doors across the room that obviously led to private offices. The doors weren't labeled, but I surmised that the one with the two-hundred-pound gorilla sitting beside it was Julio's. Renaldo tapped on the door, waited for a bark, and led us into another bare room. Total amenities were a wooden desk with one occupied chair behind it, two windows overlooking the harbor, and two vacant wooden chairs for visitors.

Julio motioned for us to sit. He was hard to study because I couldn't look at him. Every time I tried, I got pierced by a pair of black eyes that nailed me to the wall. I felt like a specimen in a butterfly collection with Julio's eyes for a pin. He reigned behind the wooden desk, which held only a green felt blotter and a manual typewriter. No papers or writing utensils were apparent.

He wore a brown suit, a wide blue tie, and a gold nugget tack. He was neat, spare, an athletic-looking sixty or more. He had lots of hair, as black as Renaldo's, slicked back in what I always thought was an Italian fashion. He was only about five-eight, but it didn't matter, he was still an imposing figure who seemed to tower over us when he got up to check his window.

I'm sure Julio knew the purpose of my visit with Renaldo was more than catching up on old times. He looked me over for a gun, which I wasn't carrying, and labeled me *bodyguard*. He must have approved of that. I didn't think the bruiser sitting in a chair outside Julio's office door with a bulge under his jacket and another on his ankle was an office boy.

I found myself wondering if there was some cat blood in Julio's family tree. A cougar or a panther a few generations back would have explained a lot about him. On second thought, I couldn't rule out a cobra, which would explain his eyes. They were the reason his flat refusal to let us visit the mine carried weight, and why my sudden resolve to visit it anyway was utterly foolhardy.

Julio got up to pace, desk to window and return, checking out the waterfront with approval, then giving me not-quite-hostile scrutiny. He didn't deny Renaldo's right to visit the mine. He put it this way; "Naturally, Renaldo, you'd be welcome to visit the mine at any other time, and bring any friends along. Right now with the shootings is not a good time. Everyone is nervous, and anything out of the routine would probably result in more shooting."

I had a feeling he was right about that, and that he wouldn't be averse to doing the shooting himself. Several times during our interview, Julio's right hand reached for a desk drawer and he had trouble pulling it back. I think his instinct was to shoot us then and there, and leaving his gun in the drawer was an act of willpower.

When we got back to Renaldo's office and closed the door, I recognized the feeling of relief. It was the same feeling I got in the second grade when my first mandatory visit to the principal's office was finally over.

Renaldo had a wooden desk, a wooden chair behind it, and an extra chair for a visitor, but we didn't sit down. One corner of the office was taken up by a steel safe the size of an apartment refrigerator. I didn't see any bookcases or ledgers. He had two windows overlooking the harbor and I gravitated that way.

"How do you transport the gold?" I wondered.

"Different ways, and no set schedule. That's part of our security precautions. Sometimes we charter an airplane, usually we put it on a ship."

"Like that ship down there?" I asked.

Renaldo came to stand beside me at his window and look down over the harbor.

"Nah, that's a cruise ship. We rarely load it on a ship here, it would be too easy for someone to hijack it. We have certain ships that we use, but no one else ever knows which ship the gold is on or when. We have our own lighter, so we can transfer shipments at sea. I keep track of where the ships are. When Julio tells me he's ready for transport, I tell him where a ship will be, offshore, or maybe even Curacao or Aruba. See, there's our lighter tied up at the third pier."

I looked, but I didn't see any lighter. Renaldo responded to my puzzled frown.

"Right there. The gray one, all by itself on the third pier over."

"Renaldo, that is not a lighter. That's a WWII torpedo boat. Didn't you ever watch McHale's Navy?"

Chapter 6

"You're going to what?" Renaldo looked up so fast that the ends of his mustache bounced, and he slammed his drink down on the table.

"Visit the mine, do your dirty work for you. Isn't that why I'm here?"

"After Julio practically promised you'd be shot?"

"You're being shot at in your living room." The window was covered, so I pointed at the chair. "How much more dangerous can the mine be?"

We'd retrieved the Jag from the parking garage and driven the six blocks back to Renaldo's aerie. (Relative to the haciendas, not the hillside.) We had both opened our car doors and scanned the domino building for rifles, then made a dignified, but hasty trip across the porch. I closed the door, but it looked flimsy, so I stepped away from it, and gave the window a wide berth, sheet cover or no. Renaldo came back from the kitchen with the appropriate brain-cell killers, and we parked at the dining table.

I raised a silent toast to show my thanks for the drink. "We need to pick up a few supplies. Visit a sporting goods store, buy some electronics, maybe get me some more-rugged shoes, stuff like that."

Renaldo returned the toast, "To your health. May it survive your incipient alcoholism and foolhardy curiosity. If you're going to the mine, how about we pick up a Sherman tank?"

"I was thinking of a more surreptitious approach. And speaking of surreptitious, maybe we shouldn't be buying the stuff I have in mind in La Guaira, just in case Julio or your assassins are keeping an eye on us."

"Don't call them my assassins."

"Okay, your new friends, whatever. How do we pick up supplies?"

"Caracas. We can run up there this evening, I just need to give Maria the night off."

"You want to walk down the road in broad daylight?"

"Maybe not, let's leave Maria a note. She plans on eating supper here and taking the leftovers home, so it'll just mean extra leftovers."

Renaldo scribbled a note for Maria, maybe not quite in the terms he'd just stated. We took a peek past the sheet at the domino building, a quick march across the porch, and after a too-fast drive down the hill, we were on our way. I glanced back every few minutes, but no one seemed to be following. After the first couple of miles the road was so crooked that I couldn't see back, and the way Renaldo was driving made it unlikely that anyone would come up behind us.

I relaxed and just enjoyed the ride and the scenery; always a mistake. We sailed around a broad curve with a five-hundred-foot drop on the left and a five-hundred-foot cliff going straight up on the right. The ubiquitous black sedan was parked crosswise in the road, and three guys were leaning across the top of it aiming rifles. I didn't see any more, I was ducked down below the dash scrabbling for the pistol in my belt. Renaldo was also down below the dash, but gripping the wheel and standing on the brake.

The windshield exploded, covering us with chunks of glass. Crackling of bullets, pings and whines all around us, and the scream from the locked-up tires were all one roar. The noise and the bullets stopped with a crash when we slammed into the sedan broadside. The gunmen were leaning over the top of the sedan and the Jag was suddenly below their line of sight. I poked my head up and was looking through the Jag's missing windshield, right through the sedan's windows at a line of three bellies. I put a bullet in each, and apparently the sedan's windows were not bulletproof, at least not to the .357 magnum. All three bellies disappeared.

Renaldo hit reverse, spun us around, and screeched back toward La Guaira just as another sedan slid broadside to block the road in that direction. I put three quick bullets into that car at no particular targets and dived over the seat to hunker down in back and reload. Renaldo was driving defensively. He slammed my head, then my posterior into opposite doors at least three times before I got the pistol reloaded. Then I had to hang on, we were sliding broadside, up on two wheels. When I managed to look up the new sedan was behind us. I had a clear view; our rear window was gone too.

Screaming tires had become the norm, and even though I was plastered against the seat, it was a second before I realized they were screaming in reverse. Three more shooters were lined up leaning over the second car. I screamed, "duck" and we both did, more crackling and pinging and whining, but no more glass to break. Renaldo slammed us right into the side of that car and I looked up when the shooting stopped, but saw no apparent targets.

The sedan threatened to roll over, teetered for a moment, but plunked back on its wheels. We seemed awfully close, so the Jag must have gotten shorter during that maneuver.

A gun came around the end of the sedan and I shot it, but we were already screaming away toward the original roadblock. Bullets started coming again, but we were weaving back and forth across the road so frantically they were missing, and I couldn't even keep track of where the car was.

"Why don't you shoot them?" Renaldo screamed.

"Because I'm using both hands to hang on."

"Good idea. Here goes." We spun broadside again, up on two wheels, within inches of the original sedan, and were turned around, but still up on two wheels when I looked straight down into hungry rocks impossibly far below us. We hung there for a lifetime before we slammed level and started that snake track back toward La Guaira. I leaned over the seat and shot in the general direction of any heads that popped up. I wasn't hitting anything or even coming close, but it did discourage them from shooting at us.

That time when we turned back toward Caracas I did shoot through their windows, but only because our passenger window suddenly angled down. We were up on two wheels again, and would have rolled, but the roof slammed into the cliff. It made a horrible screech, but held us up, and the driving tires that were still on the road were howling, so the Jag must have had positive traction. The next crash sounded like the end of the world but we didn't feel the bump. Instead of bullets, it was bits of chrome and shards of flying steel. One of the giant Mexican tour buses had come around the bend from Caracas, and you can be sure he was doing over a hundred because they always do. He slammed into the front of the car that was blocking the road and spun it halfway around. We were still up on two wheels, still ripping short shrieks of steel off the roof on rocks, when our left wheels glanced off the sedan's trunk and we were past.

Renaldo slammed us back onto four wheels and kept right on going, although the hurricane in the car had lethal chunks of glass flying around for a while. Renaldo had put on a pair of sunglasses so he could look into the slip stream from the broken windshield. He did slow us down to fifty. The ends of his mustache were wrapped around his cheeks, his hair flying behind him. I had to turn my back on the windstorm, so I kept an eye out for followers.

"Where did you learn to drive a car on two wheels?" I shouted.

"I saw it one time in a movie. I think it was Clint Eastwood, or maybe James Bond. Always wanted to try it."

We were coming into civilization, passing shantytown, when we could no longer ignore the steam that was pouring out from under the hood. Renaldo slowed us down to forty and used one hand to wipe steam off his glasses. I was sneaking quick peeks ahead expecting the hood to blow off, when the left front tire exploded.

Renaldo was holding the wheel hard right with both hands, and the ride was like I imagine a camel would be until the tire ripped off the rim with a bang. The ride smoothed out, the rim screamed on the pavement, and we kept right on going.

"Hey," I shouted. This time a shout was necessary. "You're going to ruin that rim. Shouldn't we stop and call a taxi?"

"Three more blocks. Never say die."

We made a right turn off the autopista, then a left, and slid to a stop in the parking lot of a Jaguar dealership. Renaldo climbed out, brushing off glass and went inside. I crawled out and couldn't believe what I was seeing. The car top looked as if it had been attacked with a chain saw. Doors, trunk, and hood all resembled Swiss cheese from bullet holes. The trunk lid was a foot too short and had flapped up when the car stopped. The rear bumper was almost against the rear tires, and the hiss of steam from the hood had developed an angry roar that made me step away from the car. That's when I noticed I wasn't real steady on my feet.

An overhead door opened at the side of the building and a duplicate Jag rolled out. The horn tootled. Renaldo was driving, so I wove my way over and climbed in.

"You got a new car just like that?"

"Sure, no problem. It's a company car, I just had to sign for it. Actually, they were delighted with the transaction because I didn't insist on a trade in. Where to?"

"Really clever of you to get a duplicate car, since it seems to be open season on black jaguar sedans."

We hit the electronics emporium, drapery shop, and sporting goods store. Decided against visiting Benny at the

El Conde. Naturally Renaldo suggested a favorite restaurant. Naturally he called the headwaiter by name and flirted with the waitress. After savoring the superb tarpon steaks, we headed back to La Guaira.

I kept the pistol in my hand, and Renaldo seemed to be approaching curves with more caution than usual. The ambush scene was hardly recognizable; just a smattering of glass across the road, a solid paving of rubber from the Jag's tires, and a few small car parts scattered along the shoulder on the uphill side. I suspected the sedan the bus hit had been shoved off the cliff on the downhill side, and I wondered how many bodies had been slung over, but we didn't stop to check.

We made it home alive, installed our new equipment, and turned in early. I always like to get a good night's sleep when I expect to get shot the next day.

Chapter 7

Renaldo parked the new Jag on the shoulder of Libertador Vargas. We got out, stretched our legs, and admired the vista of mountains and canyons. The view didn't include any people, so I stepped over the guardrail and slid thirty feet down in loose rocks before I caught a tree and sat down behind it. Renaldo climbed back into the Jag and drove away.

I had convinced Renaldo that carrying a gun didn't equate with barbarism. He picked out a .25 caliber Beretta automatic that fit in his jacket pocket. We stopped on that dirt road at the top of the hill outside La Guaira, and I made him fire a clip and reload it himself. He managed to get all the bullets in front of him, and didn't blow off any toes.

We had replaced the sheet over the living room window with a good heavy drape, and stuck a video camera up on the side of the house on the kitchen end. By tuning the TV to

Channel 3, he could see his car and the front porch and lawn. I was sure that would be his favorite program in future. It beat Daffy Duck and Lucille Ball speaking Spanish. We even instituted a new regimen of locking the door, and Renaldo had a key made to give Maria. We decided we didn't need to worry about him once he got to work.

What I wanted to do was get a look at the mine. I didn't think the reason for the shootings was in La Guaira. The mine didn't seem a heck of a lot more likely, but what other options were there? I had no intention of stealing any gold or crossing any *Will Be Shot* corridors. I just wanted to watch the mine a while and see what could be seen from a safe distance.

Renaldo had drawn a rough circle over the Quebrada Guemai on a road map, dropped me off on the edge of the circle, and promised to come back and pick up hitchhikers in three days. It sounded pretty simple until I got a look at Quebrada Guemai.

Quebrada means gorge, and if that chasm I was looking down was a quebrada, they probably would have called the Grand Canyon of the Colorado a quebradita. I could see a white string here and there between trees at the bottom of the gorge that might have been the headwaters of the Tacagua River.

Renaldo's map had a black line that might have denoted something like counties and it ran right through what might have been a T in what might be Tacagua. It didn't matter much. I figured if there was a mine at the bottom of that gorge, I ought to be able to find it. The first trick appeared to be getting to the bottom as a slow process rather than a one-minute flight. It wasn't the sort of cliff that would interest rappellers, but it was steeper than the average ladder, and a lot of scree appeared to be loose, just waiting for me to start a rockslide.

The fifty feet of quarter-inch nylon cord in my backpack was coiled in twenty loops. Nylon stretches like a rubber band, but it would hold several hundred pounds without breaking. A rock needle that looked like a stalagmite, except made of granite, was sticking up twenty feet below me. It took a couple of sneezes to get used to the hot dry air, and it smelled more like old birds' nests than tropical fruit.

I divided the coils of rope in half, straddled the tree with them and paid out both ends until I felt the rock behind me. I pulled one end of the rope, wrapped my rock, and spider walked across to a bush. It took three hours to work my way down to where the jungle started. Twice I found myself looking straight down for a couple of hundred feet and had to crawl back up and find another route.

Hawks, and what I think were eagles but might have been vultures, seemed to be patrolling the cliffs, circling around and around and watching to see if I was edible. They never seemed to flap their wings; they just hung as if they were suspended in a mobile.

A rockslide off to my right, where a big chunk of the rim rock had broken off and scattered itself down the slope, looked like a stream of suitcases and steamer trunks. It could have been an easy place to climb down for a while, and I worked over toward it. I was walking across a pretty good ledge, thinking "piece of cake," when I heard a whoosh behind me and ducked. What felt like a twenty-pound sledgehammer glanced off my backpack and knocked me sprawling. I grabbed a crack in the rock to keep myself on the ledge and looked up in time to see an owl the size of a turkey peel out and circle for another run at me. I was still watching him when his Mrs. raked a swath across my pack with two-inch talons. The blast of air from her passage slammed my nose against the rock, but I'd been hugging the rock pretty close anyhow, so it wasn't much of a bump.

Turning around and making a hasty retreat back along my shelf seemed to be indicated. I had no interest in discovering any owl's nest. The first attacker finished his circle and started his bombing run. He was gray, and looked cubicle, like a flying boxcar. His wings were just a blur, but I had the impression of a three-foot span. The Japanese could have gotten the idea for Kamikaze bombers from this guy.

He made a shallow dive to pick up speed and was doing about a hundred. I half stood up to meet him and stared into a big pair of malevolent yellow eyes that held every intention of killing me. I may have had some thought of fending him off with my arms, but at the last second he swung out a set of talons that looked like saucers with razor blades protruding and aimed them straight at my face. I ducked sideways and down, as if dodging a haymaker in a boxing match, and the owl whistled past my ear. He pounded me on the head with wings, but those were survivable. Thank heaven for a college education. In fact, the duck and weave from winters on the boxing team might be the only useful things I learned in college, and I credited them with saving my life.

I scrabbled another 20 feet away from the nest before Momma came around again. She must have decided my intentions were honorable and didn't make her dive, but those two oversized bumble bees circled and watched until I had scrambled 50 yards away and worked down another 20 feet.

The trees started sparsely at first, and I just slid from tree to tree; then they got serious and matted together with vines and brush. After that it was as hard to pull myself down as it had been to work back up earlier. A lot of squawking and cawing was coming from the trees. It sounded like the aviary at the San Diego zoo, and my intrusion didn't seem to bother it much.

I caught glimpses of reds and blues, greens brighter than the trees, and yellows here and there. I noticed a line of bananas along a tree branch, and when I looked again a pair of eyes stared around the top of every banana. They turned their backs and flew away.

All the bright colors didn't seem to fit with the theory of natural adaptation. In Alaska, most birds and animals are colored to match their backgrounds, so if they don't move, they're practically invisible. Several even change colors, brown in summer and white in winter. Nature makes some mistakes, particularly in autumn. Around Fairbanks, I've seen the woods suddenly full of pure white snowshoe hares that had changed color a couple weeks before the snow fell. Sometimes it happens to ptarmigan, too.

Ptarmigan are pure white birds all winter, invisible in the snow, and spend their summers as brown willow grouse blending with the trees. Maybe biologists know what triggers the color change. Maybe it's the shortening of daylight, or the drop in temperature. Perhaps premature color changes aren't a mistake at all. The camouflage gets out of sync just at harvest time when both men and wolves are fattening themselves up for winter, so maybe it's part of a master plan.

Anyhow, these jungle birds weren't much concerned with camouflage, and judging by the racket going on, they weren't much endangered. I know in some animals, bright colors are for sexual attraction, so maybe these birds were like people, putting sex ahead of safety.

The best going was through bamboo thickets, although the bamboo grew as thick as grass on a lawn. I think it might actually be a form of prehistoric, dinosaur-sized joint grass. In the thickets, stalks grew so close together that they shaded and strangled everything else. I got through it by bending the stalks aside and climbing between them. The stalks ranged in diameter from one to six inches, and up to three inches they bent pretty easily. I wasn't necessarily standing on the ground at all times, but the hardest part was making sure my pack frame got through the holes before they snapped shut. I did a lot of breath holding because the ground was usually buried under dead stalks and the mold spores made a yeasty cloud when I disturbed them.

In Tarzan movies, the jungle has big trees spaced out with vines hanging down for swinging. In this jungle, the trees almost touched each other, and the vines grew sideways to lace them together. Any space that wasn't taken up by vines was taken up by spider webs, and the occasional spider I spotted was the size of a saucer. I kept checking to make sure the vines weren't snakes.

Phase Three of my plan involved climbing back out of that gorge, but I was counting on Phase Two to be some help. If a mine down there had a couple hundred men lugging out sacks of gold, there had to be a road and a heck of a lot easier way up than the one I was taking down.

The fact that the road didn't show on Renaldo's map only meant that it was a private road, as it should be. I was taking the hard way down on the assumption that I'd probably get shot on the road, but might get pretty close to the mine from the back side. They wouldn't expect anyone to come from the wrong way, and I wasn't passing any trails made by hoards of trespassers.

A rock the size of an RV stuck up on end above the trees and I climbed up, partly to look around, and partly to get a breath of air with no leaves or webs in it. I ate a couple of fun-sized Snickers bars before I doused myself again with Deep Woods Off. A squadron of butterflies twinkled by. They were as big as bats, mostly white, but hand painted in acrylics.

Below me, the tops of trees looked like a scruffy lawn in San Francisco or Seattle where the yards stand on edge. I couldn't see the river anymore, but there was very little chance of going the wrong way. I also didn't see any mines or any roads, and in fact, no possible way for a road to get down there.

Renaldo's mine location was based on a conversation he'd had some time back with Julio. As comptroller, Renaldo had purchased the property but had never visited it and couldn't remember the coordinates.

To quote Renaldo exactly, "Julio said the mine is right there." Renaldo stuck his finger on the map and drew a circle around his finger. The circle started at the Libertador Vargas Highway where Renaldo had dropped me and included three miles of canyon. It also included a tributary coming in from my left, but all I could see up that way was a solid rock wall.

Rivers have been making highways for people, probably since Adam and Eve left the garden following the Tigris or Euphrates, or wherever the heck they were. I had faith that the stream at the bottom of that gully would do the same for me, if I could get to it. About 50 yards farther, there was a crack in the rocks above me. I say farther because I was going a lot more sideways than down, and I was instinctively heading southeast, away from the highway and deeper into Renaldo's circle.

That crack in the rock looked like a place where there would be a waterfall if it rained, and the hillside had a crease running down from it. Angel Falls is supposed to be the highest waterfall in the world, over 3,000 feet, and it's somewhere in Venezuela. It looked as if this one might be as high during a downpour.

I decided against having one more candy bar because my hands were covered with insect repellent, and I could already taste the stuff even without putting it near my mouth. I climbed down from my rock and swam through the brush toward the dry waterfall. Water hadn't made a path through the jungle, but it had made a tunnel. I took off my pack, held it against my chest and scooted right along down that tunnel under the jungle.

At first I used my feet to pull myself along, and branches and vines were within easy reach. About the time I started picking up momentum and didn't need to pull anymore, the path widened and the trees were out of reach. I tried to backpedal, but rocks and dirt were scooting right along with me. It was like floating down a millrace, except in rocks and dirt instead of water, and it sounded like the hiss ice makes crashing down a river at breakup time.

I was remembering newsreel pictures of Olympic bobsled races when I went off the ski jump. I flew up for a while, and then out for a while, and landed with a splash, sitting in a foot of water at least as cold as the Kuskokwim.

I just sat there, wondering if I was alive, while the rocks and dirt poured down the slide and piled on top of me.

My only obvious injury was a low fire, like a rope burn, on my posterior, which fortunately was packed in what felt like ice. I washed the repellent off my hands, dug the debris out of my eyes, and had one more Snickers bar before I got up. My backpack, sitting on my lap, was fine. Only the bottom, and therefore my sleeping bag, was getting wet. I took a deep breath and stood up.

The stream was a foot deep, except for deeper holes behind the bigger rocks. The water was rushing right along and was mostly white; just the sort of place to find trout in the Cascades or the Rockies. I wondered if they had trout here, or would they have goldfish, or maybe piranhas? I stood on top of a dry rock to put my pack on.

I sloshed up the stream toward the center of Renaldo's circle. I learned real soon that the roughest water was the place to walk. Sometimes it was only a couple inches deep and not much worse than walking on a cobblestone street. I'd gone at least a mile and rounded a bend when the canyon narrowed right to the edge of the stream, and the stream itself got narrower and deeper. I finally had to get out of the water and climb over rocks along the edge.

The rock walls above me made walking beside my creek like walking up Wall Street would be, if Wall Street were only one lane wide and the sidewalk had been hit by a magnitude ten earthquake or a city maintenance crew. The canyon funneled right down to sheer rock walls ten feet apart that went up forever. A cascade of water four feet high was pouring through the gap above me like the stream from a teakettle spout.

The way those walls closed in and shut out the sunlight reminded me of Hobbits and Gollum caves. No fortuitous rocks stuck out in the middle of that waterfall. I was on the left bank and couldn't see around the corner past the wall ahead, but looking across the creek, I could see that a valley opened out just past my floodgate.

A rock, a little larger than a refrigerator, sat on dry ground across the creek just a few feet upstream from the notch, and twenty feet from me. It wasn't exactly Gibraltar, but it looked like a few hundred pounds of solid granite. I stood on the last ledge, took off my pack, and dug out the rope.

I was tossing the rope over the waterfall, trying to lasso the rock on the upstream side, so every time my lasso missed, the water grabbed it and whipped it downstream so hard it felt as if a salmon was on it. I pulled it back up, squeegeed the water out, opened my loop wider, and tossed again, and again.

"If at first you don't succeed," you're going to get an awful lot of cold water down your sleeves. Finally my loop went right past the rock and dragged back without closing. When the loop dropped around the rock and pulled tight, I was so surprised I nearly pulled myself off my perch on the ledge.

I used ten feet of my end of the rope to wrap my backpack up like a cocoon and give it a leader like a kite. I set it on my ledge and left it there. I took the belly of the rope and climbed back over rocks downstream until I could get into the water without jumping. Between the spray from my little waterfall and the dripping from the rope, I really didn't have to worry about getting wetter. Colder was another matter.

Pulling myself up the center of the current seemed like it just might work. The water was shoving me up like a water skier, so I was practically on top of it. I pulled myself right along to the bottom of the waterfall. At that point the rope was under water, or under the falls, and my water ski suddenly turned into a submarine.

The water must have shoved me down ten feet, and I hung onto the rope for dear life, literally, I expect. Suddenly the water threw me sideways, and I fetched up against the opposite bank with a whack that rattled my bones. The rope pulled me back to the surface, and I just hung on and breathed for a while.

From my new perspective against the right bank, I could see past the wall where my perch had been and where my pack was still sitting. It looked like warm sunshine on Elysian Fields just 40 feet away. I noticed I was shivering, and my hands weren't quite right, getting stiff with the cold. If I'd been thinking, I would have climbed out and warmed up, but I got a now-or-never feeling and pulled myself back toward the waterfall.

With me on the same side as my anchor, the rope was pulled tight against the side of the spout and the water shoved me against the rocks. I easily kept my head up until I went under the falls again. The pressure still shoved down, but my belly against the side helped hold me. I was down pretty deep, but I kept grabbing more rope and it kept going by.

The downward pressure stopped, the weight on my back doubled, but it was shoving me sideways against the rock. I got a burn on my belly to match my backside, but I broke the surface on the uphill side of the waterfall. I kept pulling myself hand over hand up the rope until I noticed I was out of the water, lying on dry ground. I just sprawled there and choked and gasped until I felt the sun work through my wet crust and seep into my bones.

It was a jungle-filled valley instead of a rocky gorge. Walls were still just as high, but they made sloping sides like a soup bowl instead of the sheer drops. The bowl held a good bit of jungle and the rim was still rock, but the jungle sloped up so the rock rim was a hundred feet tall instead of thousands. I scanned and found no sign of any road or any mine. My raging cataract was a gentle millpond from this perspective. Fifty yards up the valley, it turned into a meandering stream with nice dry dirt on both sides.

My anchor rock was the only handy high spot. Standing on top of it gave me an upward angle and I pulled in slack until the rope ran straight from me to my pack. When the belly of the rope went under the falls it pulled pretty hard, but the pressure was down on the edge of the shelf on the other side so it didn't drag my pack off.

I leaned forward, wrapped the rope around my hand, and jerked. The pack jumped off the ledge, hit the top of the waterfall, and skipped across the water like the flat stones we used to skip when we were kids. We would count the skips and compete for the most. My pack only took six skips, far from a record, but very gratifying.

The pack was soaked. I emptied it out and spread things around on the rock to dry. Then I stripped, wrung out my clothes, and spread them, too. I didn't have anything dry to use for a towel so I sat on my rock and shivered while the sun evaporated the water.

I think it was Amundsen who saved his life that way in the arctic. He fell through the ice into the Arctic Ocean, and when he came up, he stripped and wrung things out. His companions thought he'd lost his mind and tried to stop him, but he stood there on the ice and snow, temperature probably below zero, and calmly put his wrung-out clothes back on. That image made my ordeal seem survivable.

The pistol was inside a Ziplock bag and dry. Those horrible commercials with the bag full of bees were apparently right. I treated my exclusive little nudist colony to a can of mushroom soup. I didn't worry about a campfire and boiling water. I just opened the can with my knife and ate the thick paste inside with a plastic spoon. That may not sound good, but don't knock it until you've tried it. A lot of food is concentrated there, it tastes just fine, and the mushrooms are great. I was just sorry I didn't have any crackers to go with it.

Chapter 8

By the time I was packed and walking beside the stream, it was late afternoon. My duffle and I had been dry for a while, but it had felt good sitting on my rock. There's a feeling of freedom to lounging in the sunshine naked, and I could understand the lure of nudist colonies. It was the sun disappearing from the valley floor that got me started.

The strip of hard dry ground beside the creek that made walking easy wouldn't be there after a rainstorm. With a good gully-washer rain and a flash flood, the creek would reach jungle to jungle, but with low water, it left a nice clear path for hiking.

To justify just sitting on the rock, I had pretended to think. My idea was to find the mine and an observation point before dark and watch the mine all night. In my experience, when people get shot the underlying causes are frequently nocturnal. If the mine just sat there dormant, as it should, until the miners shouldered their picks in the morning, it would neutralize some of the suspicions that were beginning to nag me.

From Renaldo's description, I was picturing a cleared corridor around the mine, like an Alaska firebreak line. To be effective, it should be lighted at night, so I was expecting a scene like a sports arena lit up for a nighttime game. It should be easy enough to spot, if not to cross.

A sudden movement in peripheral vision had me diving for the ground and whipping the gun out of my belt. I saw the sentry crouched in a tree. He was dressed in brown, just a little too light for perfect camouflage, and he had white markings on his face like an Apache warrior in paint. I didn't see any gun, and when I stopped moving, I started to see more men in the trees, all sitting perfectly still and eyeing me. Suddenly one of them screamed, exactly like the wicked witch in *The Wizard of Oz*. They all started screaming and chattering, and swung away through the trees, using long thin arms and tails.

I put the gun away and swiped some of the fresh mud off my knees. The heavy pair of dungarees and long-sleeved shirt I was wearing had been laundered pretty well by the waterfall, so I was starting over clean, but I had quite a few rips and tears here and there.

An hour of gentle climbing led to the end of my valley, this time with no theatrics. It sloped up for a couple of hundred feet while the creek boiled down a rock ladder. The valley ahead narrowed, but to a hundred feet instead of ten like the waterfall. I topped the rise and looked into another bowl. This one had a good-size lake lapping against the lower rim.

There appeared to be some branches from this valley but it was hard to see just what was there, and I realized that was because it was getting dark, fast.

I had to choose between rushing ahead, hoping to find the mine before dark, or using the last of the daylight to set up a camp. I chickened out and found a hole in the edge of the jungle where a stream and an ancient landslide had piled up a bunch of boulders. A flat rock, big enough to lay out the sleeping bag, looked promising. Beside it, a crevice between rocks might be deep enough to hide a campfire.

A racket was still coming from the trees. Squawks and whistles were so constant that I tuned them out, and the occasional scream wasn't making me jump anymore. Splashes were coming from the lake, and half circles spreading out from the banks rippled in the fading light, but I couldn't see what was making them.

I took off the pack, scurried around gathering twigs and branches, and settled down on my rock bed by the time it was too dark to see the lake. I unrolled the sleeping bag, sat on it and hugged my knees while the eastern rim of the valley disappeared in darkness. If there was a sunset, I didn't see it. The light just went out, and the few stars that showed up for nightlights were dim and out of focus. The inconstant moon that had lighted the terrain a few nights ago was missing. The air was clear of any normal man-made pollutants, but had too much water in it for stargazing.

The cool night air made me grateful for my windbreaker and I had to wonder about that because I'd been in a steam bath most of the day, when I wasn't freezing in the creek. It should be cool on top because the cliffs were three and four thousand feet high, but with my valley walls almost that high, I must have been sitting near sea level. La Guaira, at sea level, was much warmer than Caracas, and both were warmer than my valley.

It occurred to me finally that warm air rises and cold air sinks, and my valley was filling up with the coldest. I stuck my legs inside the bag and set my pack behind me for a backrest. I wasn't in any hurry to light a fire because, shielded or not, it would show up like a beacon in that dark valley. So would any lights around a mine or a road, and I wanted them to show first, if they were there.

I tried to think about Renaldo's problem, but my mind kept coming back to the girl on the hillside, earning ten thousand Bolivars a week. That's about nineteen dollars and a dime, and I couldn't imagine anyone living on that, let alone staying sharp and beautiful. Maybe she had a husband, and six teenage kids, all of them earning money, but that thought didn't fit my fantasy, so I kicked it out.

Two hours crept by and no light appeared in the valley. The jungle seemed to be going to sleep. A tiny smudge of light overhead was the only assurance that I hadn't gone blind. I suspected it was Jupiter, but there was nothing to put it in perspective. I felt inside my pack for the baggie that held the lighter and my penknife.

Mostly to kill some more time, I felt for a nice dry stick a little thicker than my thumb and spent some time making a shaving stick out of it. That was a legacy from the year I misspent as a Boy Scout. You slice shavings on the end of the stick, but you don't cut them off, so the end of your stick looks like a feather duster.

When I snapped the lighter under the stick, it was blinding, like a naked thousand-watt bulb, until my eyes readjusted. I stuck it down in my crevice and leaned twigs against it on end to make an Indian fire. The sobriquet "Indian fire" came from the saying, "White man build big fire, can't get near it. Indian build little fire, sit on top." I don't know where that came from, more likely from the Boy Scouts than from Sitting Bull.

I dug out the can of beef stew by its shape—short and wide—and opened the lid most of the way, but left it attached to make a handle. It fit the crack in the rocks above my fire, and it smelled like Sunday dinner at Grandma's house. You can eat the stew cold because it's fully cooked, but the grease congeals, and it's much nicer hot.

When it bubbled, I used my handkerchief for a hot pad to grab the lid and set the can on the rock. I dug in with the same plastic spoon I'd used on the mushroom soup. The stew struck me as superb. I couldn't cut the chunks of beef with the spoon, so I stuck them in my mouth whole and didn't mind a bit.

I might have felt substandard heating cans over a fire like a swagman with his billy boiling. The new ideal is the super light freeze-dried trail foods packed in foil for mountain climbers. They are easier to carry, and much classier, but I've been there and done that. Besides being ridiculously expensive, they require water and utensils. Water is the toughest commodity to get in a survival situation. You can try melting snow, but if it's cold, it takes a bucket full of snow to make a cupful of water.

A pristine mountain lake was lapping fifty feet away. I'd use it before I died of thirst, but only if I could boil it for twenty minutes. A lot of people think that if you get away from civilization you get away from pollution, but that's not the case. Maybe I shouldn't be speaking for Venezuela, but in Alaska bears and moose do the most disgusting things in streams, and beavers and salmon die in them. I've picked a heck of a lot more hunters off of sandbars because they had acute giardia than because they shot themselves in the foot.

I chased the stew with a slug of bottled water and screwed the cap back on. I slid the pack from a backrest to a pillow and zipped the bag up tight. At first it was reminiscent of my claustrophobic jet ride. I seemed to have a lot of muscles I'd never noticed before. You can't really stretch in a sleeping bag, but I worked at it, and apparently went to sleep.

The jungle commenced to squawk and howl. The sky got light a long time before the air got warm, so I stayed in the bag and pretended to study the terrain for a while. For breakfast I ate two Snickers bars and had a drink of water. That's probably not healthy, and it certainly isn't classy; it's just what I do when I'm on a long walk and living out of a packsack. After all, I wasn't in that valley for my health. I was in the valley for Renaldo's health, and he was probably having eggs Benedict at the moment.

The tributary on the map came into the valley in a gorge like a thumb sticking out of a mitten. I followed the thumb until noon, climbing over rocks, ripping through vines, wading through pools. The gorge ended in a hundred-foot waterfall, with no mines around. I backtracked and followed the main stream up through two more valleys.

I spent the night on a patch of grass beside a rockslide. The jungle switched to nighttime mode, quieter but far from silent. Most of the sounds were soothing except for the occasional scream when some nocturnal hunter got lucky. I tuned it all out and let it blend until an amorous cricket started bleating an unrequited love song. For a while the cricket was nice and woodsy, even musical, but after a couple of hours his chirps were like the Chinese water torture.

Again, my tiny fire between two rocks was the only light in the universe. I had canned tamales and capped them with a little plastic cup of tapioca pudding. I was scheduled to meet Renaldo on the highway the next afternoon, so my plan to spend the night watching the mine had, as Robert Burns predicted, "gang agley."

By noon the next day I'd had enough. For one thing, I'd almost doubled the size of Renaldo's circle. For another, a creek came in from the left, which was the direction of the highway, and it made a reasonable rockslide to climb up out of the valley. According to the map, the highway had been paralleling me the whole time, a mile or two from the canyon. If I'd counted the streams right, this one led right past the highway and would make an easy way to get through the jungle.

Easy is a relative term. I climbed over rocks and waded through pools. I even considered swinging across a pool on a vine, but decided I'd wade across to begin with, rather than after the vine broke. By four o'clock, I was lying in the brush beside the road, and at five-fifteen the Jaguar came sizzling up the highway. I jumped out and waved. Renaldo drove by, then braked and backed up.

"Sorry, I didn't recognize you. You look like a terrorist who forgot to let go of the bomb."

I opened the car door. From his shocked expression, I thought he was going to drive away again.

"Hey, be careful how you sit, try not to touch the upholstery, don't even think about putting those boots on the floor mats."

"Screw you," I said. I leaned back in the soft seat and closed my eyes.

"You didn't find the mine, did you?"

"What makes you think that?"

"You've got that same woebegone expression you had after every date in college."

"Renaldo, there isn't any mine. You imagined it. I'm the first person who's ever been in the bottom of that canyon, and the last person who ever will be."

"You didn't like the facilities at the campgrounds? No paper in the privies, trails a little rough, what?"

"Renaldo, there isn't a single Coke can or cigarette butt in that canyon. I think it might be a different planet down there." I gave him a couple of simulated snores to emphasize my immediate intentions.

"Hey, don't go to sleep yet. I've got a nice surprise for you."

I opened one eye, half way. Renaldo had turned around and headed back toward the Autopista Caracas-La Guaira. We'd traveled a mile when he pointed off to the left toward the mercifully hidden gorge. A dirt road led into the jungle and a sign said, "No Trespassing, mining and blasting area." It was repeated in Spanish. Renaldo slowed down.

"Sorry, Julio never mentioned a driveway. Shall I drop you here?"

"You've got to be kidding."

"Well, you're already camouflaged. You could pass for a dung heap anywhere."

"Home, James. Shower, shave, rum, bed. After that, a night of passionate love making with a movie star and a week at the resort on Aruba. Then, maybe I'll think about passing for a dung heap again." I went to sleep and dreamed about crickets chirping.

Chapter 9

I worked through my agenda, right up to the movie star. I was dreaming about her, and she looked a lot like the jewelry counter girl from the tin hut. Something clanged on the roof. I found myself standing naked in the middle of the bedroom floor with the pistol in my hand. The bang was followed by scraping and sliding noises like a body being dragged down the front half of the metal roof.

My old purple robe was hanging on the doorknob. I grabbed it and belted it while I ran down the stairs barefoot. The sound of the dragging body got to the porch at the same time I got to the window. I peeked around the drape in time to see a rock the size of a grapefruit fall past the porch and roll across the lawn. It teetered on the edge of the lawn, fell into the road, and rolled across to disappear down toward the mansion below.

When I started back up the stairs, I could see prints of

my bare feet in dust. In the bathroom, the towel on the rack was the one I'd used the night before, and I didn't much want to use it again. The linen closet in the bathroom had no clean towels. I got one of my brilliant ideas that will make me rich and famous someday when the world discovers me.

I walked up the hill and identified Maria's house by the contraption Renaldo and I had climbed up. The scene on the verandah was the same, except that the firing squad had been replaced by two cardboard boxes. I watched the boxes for a moment and decided they were bulldozers, digging a mine, or maybe making a highway through mountains. Juan Jr.'s bulldozer needed a new muffler. His little apple cheeks were puffed out and vibrating so fast they were blurred.

Maria dropped her knitting and rushed, but she shook my hand instead of kissing me, and Juan was right behind her with his two-handed shake again. He smiled that toothpaste ad and put his finger to his forehead to make shooting gestures, but he wasn't threatening me, just reliving old times. Maria's parents smiled and nodded their toothless welcomes.

After a brief conference, Maria and I climbed the stairs up the hill together. Maria stopped on the landing to look back and embrace the scene, arms wide. She pulled the panorama against her bosom, pretty much the way she embraced Renaldo. I could understand the feeling.

"Twelve thousand bolivars a week," I said. I thought it was diplomatic to offer a housekeeper less than the cook was earning. Maria's nod seemed affirmative.

"And she can have that bedroom under the stairs." The hesitation before the nod was barely perceptible.

I stopped on the path at the scene of my first encounter

with the lovely lady. Maria sauntered on down the path, tapped on the roofing, and disappeared inside. Quite a lot of vehement Spanish came out through the entry. I was expecting to hear slaps and screams, but Maria came out unscathed, and two steps behind her, my vision reappeared.

The vision wore the same outfit, obviously just back from the cleaners. She carried a bedroll under one arm and had a little suitcase in her other hand. The case was about as battered as mine and the size that I think is called *overnight*. I stayed on the path, so we bunched up for the introduction. Maria kept it simple.

"Alex, Paloma."

I reached to take the case. Paloma jerked it back and cocked it, ready to brain me with it if I reached again. I took the hint and led the way back to the stairs. We walked together down to Maria's landing. Maria caught my arms, maybe to keep my hands to myself, and gave me a peck on the cheek before she turned toward the juvenile construction site.

Paloma and I continued down the road. She stayed one step behind, and well out of reach. She followed me up the stairs into the house with the same posture and enthusiasm that French queens must have used on their way to the guillotine. I opened the door to the spare room and gestured an imaginary red carpet. She marched in and closed the door, rather pointedly.

I went foraging for breakfast, drained the coffee pot and started a fresh one. Opening the drapes in the living room seemed safe enough in the daytime and the sunshine was cheerful. No rifles protruded from the Domino Building. I'd thought about booby trapping the shooter's blind, or maybe nailing plywood over the windows, but there must have been thirty other rooms in that building that would do just as well.

The 1967 almanac was still on the chair where the dummy had dropped it when he got shot. We had left the chair, but no one had been inclined to sit in it. I looked up Venezuela in the almanac. It listed an amazing amount and variety of agricultural exports for a country with only 3% arable land. Exports included petroleum, aluminum, iron, steel, cement, and illicit drugs. It listed Venezuela as an important money-laundering hub. I wondered how those statistics were compiled. I didn't doubt them, I just wondered.

The almanac also said that the primary cash crop of California was illicit cannabis. I wondered if someone should send a copy of the almanac to the DEA. However, it seemed obvious that if the "war on drugs" were won, then the richest member of the United States would go broke. If that happened, where would the money come from to fund the DEA? It did seem to me that somebody was kidding somebody.

Paloma came out of her room at a quarter to twelve, still in the same outfit. Apparently she wasn't giving up her day job. I was happy to note that she wasn't carrying her suitcase. She tried to get past without looking at me, but I stepped in front of her and forced a house key and a twenty-dollar bill into her hands. She still made it out of the house without looking at me. She wasn't wearing a scent, so the perfume must have come from the store. Maybe it was a sample from the cosmetic counter.

I would have given a lot to take a look in her room, but I couldn't do it. It would have been such a profound invasion of her privacy that if I did, I'd be the one not looking at

All that Glisters // 93

her. Instead, I took a walk back up the hill. Her lean-to was not the hidden entrance to an underground palace. What was there was exactly what appeared from the trail.

Five sheets of tin roofing were overlapped and dug into the hillside top and bottom. Another sheet was jammed in sideways across the back. The floor was hard-packed dirt, but it was swept clean. Sweeping a dirt floor clean may sound like a contradiction, but it was clean, and the sweeping instrument was the only object left inside. It was a badly worn-out broom with a broken handle leaning against the back corner, apparently left for the next tenant. "House for lease; partly furnished."

I walked back down the hill and rubbernecked my way through town all the way to the waterfront. The outstanding feature at the moment was a brilliant white cruise ship anchored in the middle of the harbor. The smokestacks identified Sitmar, an Italian line, but the name of the ship, *Fair Sea*, was in English, and the tourists being lightered back and forth looked American.

The little boats were discharging brightly colored shirts and hats, about twenty at a time, into waiting tour buses. Four boat loads of tourists filled each bus, and they were rushed to Caracas so they wouldn't spend any money in La Guaira.

Piers held the usual assortment of fishing boats, homemade yachts, tugboats, and derelicts. My interest was at the third pier, but I didn't want to be obvious about it. The third was the only pier with just one boat. A sign next to the sidewalk read "*Prohibido*." I decided not to pretend that I didn't know what that meant. I leaned against the railing for a while, enjoyed the sun and the sea breeze, and watched a ragged, barefoot chap, who appeared to be in his sixties, fish for flounder.

I couldn't see anyone on the PT boat, but I never doubted that someone was there, probably several someones. I don't know how it is that an inanimate object can appear to be evil, but this one did. In McHale's Navy, the same vessel looked cute and cuddly. In Kennedy's story, PT-109 looked businesslike and professional. This one looked decidedly sinister. Maybe it was the canvas-covered machine guns still mounted on the cabin and the deck. They looked out of place beside the tourists and the old fisherman.

The fisherman reeled in a flounder and dropped it on the sidewalk. It flopped around, both eyes on top and looking for the ocean, which it wasn't going to find. The big fisherman was going to eat the little fish, just as they have since time began. This is a cruel world, and *pity* is a four-letter word. Start feeling for creatures lower on the food chain and you'll turn into a wild-eyed vegetarian pacifist.

I looked up toward the windows of Renaldo's office. I couldn't see him, but he was sitting up there, a small fish in the great scheme of things. My job was to identify and maybe de-fang the shark that was nibbling at him. I know, sharks don't have fangs, but that's how I viewed the situation.

Chapter 10

"Dum-de-ump-ump, dum-de-ump-ump, dum-de-ump-ump, dum." Why the heck should Vivaldi's *Four Seasons* be running through my head now? I was crawling through the jungle on my belly, using my elbows for locomotion like a seal uses his flippers, but I was a lot slower. Renaldo's raingear slid through the brush pretty well, but it was hotter than an Eskimo steam bath.

The raingear was one of those rubber outfits, pants and jacket, dark brown, but just a little too shiny for perfect camouflage. I had the cuffs and ankles taped tight to keep the bugs and brambles out, but mostly they seemed to be keeping the sweat in. I had the gun in my belt inside the raincoat, but I figured I could get to it pretty fast if the need suddenly arose. The rest of my supplies were candy bars and a flask of water in my pockets. It would be impossible to drag a pack through this jungle.

Renaldo was to pick me up around noon the next day, only twenty hours away, so there was no need to carry a cook shack with me. I was crawling on an angle, away from the highway toward the "No Trespassing, blasting area" driveway. If my path was straight, I'd meet the driveway half a mile from the road. I don't mean straight-straight because I was crawling around a different tree or bush every three feet, but the average might be all in one direction.

You can't stand up and fight your way through the jungle because it's too thick, but if you keep your nose in the mud, you can crawl under it. The trees I was crawling around were mostly palms, but there was an eclectic mix of nut trees and various relatives of alders. Those were not a problem. Tarzan could have swung through those. It was the smaller trees that filled the spaces in between that made walking impossible.

The most prolific trees were the ones called tangan tangan in the Pacific. They have lacy little leaves like a locust, but they're a hundred times tougher, with flat brown pea pods and thorns on them. The whole mess was woven together by a kind of ivy with big split leaves like a philodendron. It went right up the trees and stuck roots into the bark as it went, so you could cut it off, but still not pull it loose. One vine that seemed to wander up and down and sideways, indiscriminately, looked like a two-inch hawser, but it had purple flowers like hollyhocks every few feet.

I wasn't the only thing crawling through the jungle. The birds were only half as numerous as they had been in the gorge, and these were a lot quieter. The other crawlers were smaller, some furry, some scaly, and so far, all of them shy. Gnats and mosquitoes were not shy, but my hands and face were the only exposed flesh and those were generously

All that Glisters // 97

slathered with Deep Woods Off. I kept my lips pressed shut and tried not to breathe in gnats through my nose.

After what seemed like hours of crawling, I came to a pile of trees that had been cut and tossed around the edge of a clearing. They were jumbled every which way like the toss in a game of Pick-Up-Sticks. I took my time and wriggled through them without snapping any twigs. The clearing was a corridor forty feet wide, and beyond that an eight-foot cyclone fence surrounded a cluster of buildings. I hadn't seen any "Will be Shot" signs, but I did see a sentry shack where the driveway went through the gate.

I decided I was close enough, and settled down under a bush between the cut trees to see what happened next. My view between two logs was the front side of the compound. I was fifty feet from the right hand corner. The driveway and gate were two hundred feet to my left. My back commenced to itch like crazy. I rubbed against a tree like a horse, but carefully so the tree didn't move. That was the most exciting thing that happened for a couple of hours.

It was pretty hard to believe that there could be over a hundred men living and working on the other side of the fence. There weren't enough buildings to house that many people. The buildings were wooden clapboard, unpainted and short on windows, so I wasn't getting any clues to what was going on inside.

After a while I figured out that the mound I could see beyond the buildings was dirt, but it was covered by vines. Some serious digging and dirt piling had been done at some point, but none of it looked recent. I know vines and things grow fast in the tropics, but if they were mining every day, then rocks and dirt should be piling up every day.

By the time it got dark, I was wondering if anyone was in the guard shack. Maybe this was an abandoned site that had nothing to do with Renaldo's mine. The perimeter lights I had been expecting didn't appear, but that wasn't conclusive. The jungle itself was a pretty good barrier. This jungle was a heck of a lot quieter than the one down below, and I didn't think it was in my honor. I thought maybe I wasn't the only one there. A couple of times a bird started a ruckus and ceased or flew away in mid squawk. None of the trees around me were moving, but I kept checking.

It had taken me over two hours to crawl in from the highway, and I doubt I could have done it carrying any significant weapons. Also, the fact that it was getting hard to make out the fence in the dark did not mean that guards, if any, were blind. There might be infra red motion sensors that could see just fine. I had promised myself a look at the mine. I had not promised it would be exciting.

I wondered how Renaldo and Paloma were getting on. We had finished dinner the night before and Maria was just packing up to leave when Paloma came home. Paloma used her key and headed straight for her room, carrying a package wrapped in plain brown paper, and it looked like clothes to me.

Maria followed her into the room and dragged her back out by the wrist, sans package. Maria introduced Paloma to Renaldo. Renaldo spouted Spanish at Paloma until she smiled. It struck me that when I had met her on the trail, and when I asked her for the time at the store, she favored me with warm sunny smiles. It was only when the two of us were in the house alone that I turned into an invisible stranger.

Maria had plunked Paloma down at the table and served her a steak with mashed potatoes and a glass of wine. Paloma bowed her head in reverent silence for several seconds before she made the sign of the cross and dug into the steak. Maria gave Renaldo his kiss and skipped out. Paloma finished her dinner, took the plate to the kitchen and washed it.

Renaldo and I had pretty well figured out what was wrong with the Seattle Seahawks' strategy and were getting right along through the fresh bottles of rum and gin that Renaldo had brought home. Paloma came out of the kitchen and went straight to her room. She didn't slam the door, but she had a way of closing it that denoted finality. Maybe she was enjoying having a door; her house on the mountain didn't have one.

We finished the bottles and turned in early in preparation for our early morning departure. We had taken off before daylight to launch the excursion I was on now, so I didn't see Paloma in the morning. She would undoubtedly be at work now, and I had a strong hunch she'd be wearing a different outfit. I tried to remember the perfume she'd been wearing when I accosted her at her counter. It wasn't a particularly successful effort, but it did improve the smell of the jungle some.

My mind was jerked back to the present. The compound let out a whoop, whoop, whoop sound, low but insistent. Headlights flashed on the gate from the driveway, and suddenly the area lit up like Las Vegas. Floodlights came on in trees and the whole place looked like high noon. A stake-bed truck bombed out of the trees and stopped at the gate. It was instantly surrounded by machinegun-toting mercenaries, and they hadn't come from the guard shack. They must have been in the trees beside the driveway, because the gate to the compound was still closed.

The load in the truck was a mound in the middle of the bed, covered by a tarp. A man crouched at each of the four corners of the truck bed. Each held a weapon pointed at the sky, and they sat like statues while the sentries from the trees swarmed over the truck. Flashlights beamed into the cab and under the truck. Four men stood behind the truck with weapons at the ready while two men climbed up on the bed and removed the tarp.

I couldn't make out what the load was, but it looked to me like it might have been bales of hay. Renaldo hadn't mentioned using any mules at the mine. The men behind the truck bed trained their guns on the four who sat motionless. Those four dropped their weapons and jumped down. A whistle blew, the gate slid open, and the truck disappeared inside. The four new arrivals were marched into the guard shack, and the lights went out.

I was glad I hadn't tried to sneak down the driveway, but I was perplexed. I would have expected a heavily-armed contingent to bring out the gold. I wasn't coming up with any good reason why a shipment with armed guards should go into a gold mine.

Wasn't it Aristotle who first said, "All that glitters is not gold?" He would have said it in Latin, so if I remembered it from high school, someone had quoted it in English. Was it Silas Marner? Did Shakespeare use it? Damn, that was going to bother me all night.

In twenty minutes, the truck came out empty. The traveling guards came out of the shack and jumped up in back, but didn't pick up their weapons. The gate opened, the truck slipped away, and the mine appeared deserted again. "All that glisters..." Didn't Don Quixote say something like that?

It was after midnight when the whoop-whoop sounded again. It was a different truck, but the scene was repeated, as if it had been choreographed for a dance company.

"All that glisters is not gold, often have you heard that told." The message in Portia's golden cask, *The Merchant of Venice*. Now, can we think about something else, like the way my legs are going to sleep and I don't dare move them?

After a few eons, enough daylight woke up to show the fence and the buildings. The gate slid open two feet and two men came out. They carried weapons and walked out of sight up the drive. Five minutes later, two different men came back and went inside. Two more came out, and the shift change continued until I had counted sixteen men who were apparently stationed outside the gate and along the drive.

Men stopped coming out, but the gate stayed open. A couple of uneventful minutes dragged by before two guys came out and split to walk around the fence in opposite directions. The one coming my way held his gun at the ready and watched the jungle as he came. I got the pistol in my hand, but considering the amount of backup he had, I kept the pistol out of sight under me. I buried my nose in the leaves on the ground and hoped the slicker was dirty enough to blend in. I made like an ostrich until I heard footsteps pass. I had a feeling it wasn't over, and it wasn't. A minute later a different guy came back the other way.

The guy who came back wasn't scanning the jungle. I think he had breakfast and bed on his mind, because I'm pretty sure he had been at the back corner of the compound all night. I gave him my ostrich act anyway and kept it up until I heard the gate clang shut. I was hoping another truck would show up to make some noise so I could slip out, but none did. I had an appointment with Renaldo, and I was eager to talk to him.

I backed out of the brush an inch at a time for ten feet before I turned around and started to crawl. I might have been quiet sneaking in, but nothing like I was going out. I'd gone fifty feet when I came to a stump. That may not seem remarkable in a jungle, but it is. In the jungle things rot so fast that if it isn't growing, it isn't there. This stump had a nice clean cut, like a chain saw would make, and it didn't seem a likely place for someone to be logging.

It was sculpted and painted, so I put my hand on it before I realized it was concrete. The top was screened, and a blast of hot air coming out had a smell that reminded me of drug stores. Well, of course, mines have to have air vents. Naturally, underground the mine would reach far beyond the fence. I couldn't see any light down the hole, and all I could hear was a rumble from a fan. The vent was a fourteen-inch pipe, so I wasn't tempted to try some pot-boiler stunt of crawling down it.

I got to the edge of the road at eleven, an hour early. I took off the oilskins and scratched and danced for a while, then folded my uniform under my arm and hiked through the brush along the edge of the road toward home. I wanted to be as far as possible from that driveway with its armed guards before I met Renaldo.

I wasn't nearly as dirty as I had been on my last hitchhiking stint, and Renaldo picked me up with no complaints. He'd covered the Jag's leather seat with an old army blanket. I'd been wanting to talk to him, but when I leaned back in that seat in the gentle wash of the air conditioner, the lights went out.

Chapter 11

Dinner was a raging success. I'd eaten half a pound of Snickers bars and drunk a quart of water while I watched the mine, so I really wasn't deprived, but they were no substitute for the spread Maria laid out around a heaping bowl of paella. We didn't chat because all mouths were full at all times, and while Paloma was decorative, she seemed to have a chilling effect on socializing. The pleated white skirt and pink blouse had been replaced by a straight black skirt and a white blouse. Her blouse was off the shoulder, so she didn't have any chips on them, she just didn't seem to want to get acquainted. Since I'd already used my entire Spanish vocabulary on her, I was no help, and those elegant bare shoulders were keeping me distracted. Even Renaldo seemed subdued.

While Maria and Paloma cleared the table, Renaldo and I settled down with the balm of Gilead.

"Alex, what you saw were shipments of mercury. Mercury is used in gold mining to pick up the small stuff. I looked it up." Renaldo used the napkin off the table to daub his mustache, then used it for a coaster.

"Delivered by armed guards in the middle of the night?"

"Well, sure. Mercury is expensive. In fact, it's the biggest expense we have, right up there with payroll." Renaldo stood and picked up the empty ice bucket.

"Renaldo, mercury is used in placer mining, not hard rock."

Paloma had come out of the kitchen and closed her door for the night. I'd been happy to note that the dust was gone from the stairs, and fresh towels had proliferated in the upstairs bathroom. Maria came out of the kitchen and gave Renaldo an outrageous smooch. She even smiled at me and pecked my cheek, so maybe I was losing my ugly-American status.

Renaldo and I were working our way through a couple more bottles and watching Channel 3 on his television. The show was just the lawn and the porch, with the top of Renaldo's Jag in the foreground. I'd rate the program somewhere near the middle of the talk shows.

Renaldo came back from the kitchen with the bucket of ice, and we both mixed fresh drinks. "So, now you're an expert on gold mining?"

"No, but every spring I haul several miners into their creeks, and pick them up in the fall, so I know what they take with them."

"And, they all carry mercury, right?" We'd moved the Barcalounger over toward the side of the room, more or less out of the line of fire, and the drapes were closed tight.

Renaldo carried his drink and sat down in the lounger. He pushed back two clicks and took a sip of his gin and tonic. I scooted my chair around to face him and the TV.

"Right," I explained, "each one carries a little metal bottle of mercury that holds a pint and weighs ten pounds. The difference is that a lot of those guys are going after flour gold."

"Flower gold? You mean to make jewelry out of?"

"No, I mean flour, like in baking a cake. The gold got vaporized and spit out of volcanoes, and it settled over the whole Kilbuck Mountain Range like dust. They're picking up gold so fine that if you can see a chunk with the naked eye they consider it a nugget. When they clean up a pan, the bottom looks like it was painted yellow. They dump in a half teaspoon of mercury and roll it around the pan."

"So then the pan looks silver?" Renaldo wasn't appreciating my expertise.

"No, the gold amalgamates together with the mercury. All those heavy metals are atomically related so they form a loose bond. The glob of mercury still rolls around the pan, but after a while it starts to look lumpy and they pour that into a jar."

"If a pint lasts all summer, they must not get very much gold." Renaldo leaned back one more click in his Barcalounger.

"Maybe not by your standards, but those guys head for Florida or Arizona for the winter, and they talk about their swimming pools and speed boats. They have a special lid for the jars that looks like an oilcan spout coming off sideways. When the jar of amalgam gets a little full, they screw this special lid on and warm up the jar by a campfire.

They dribble water on the spout to keep it cool. The mercury boils right off the gold and drips out of the spout back into the original bottle."

"Hey, maybe we should try that. It might save the company a pile of money." That was the first time Renaldo appeared interested in my mining seminar, but I had to barge ahead and break his bubble.

"Well, that's the other thing. I don't think mercury is very expensive. I think they take small amounts just because it's heavy to carry. Back during the Alaska gold rush, mercury was so cheap that the miners sprinkled it on the ground before they started to pan. I know of a couple of greenhorns who almost had heart attacks because they thought they had discovered platinum. They panned for gold and got shiny silver metal, but it was gold covered with mercury that was dumped all those years ago."

A flicker of movement on the television caught our attention. When we looked nothing was there, but we zeroed in on the TV and forgot about mining. The Jaguar's hood raised up into the picture.

"Hey, someone's stealing my car!" Renaldo jumped up to run for the door, but I shoved him back into his lounger.

"Don't go near the door if you like living." I scooped the .357 off the table beside me and dived into Renaldo's bedroom. The window at the end of the room was already open. I unhooked the screen and dropped down into the bushes, surviving with minimal scratches. I crawled along behind the hibiscus hedge past the end of the lawn, and slid down to the road.

A streetlight a block away on the corner made the road seem too light, but the lawn terrace was between me and the

Jaguar thief. I crouched and slipped toward the driveway. Suddenly a pair of headlights came on fifty yards up the road, and tires screamed, straight toward me. The headlights silhouetted the gun sights, and I shot out both lights so I could see again. The car was still coming fast and there was no place to run. The bank on my right was ten feet high, straight up, and the left side of the road dropped into eternity.

I shot three times, under the car near the end of the chrome bumper. The third shot blew the car's right front tire. The car swerved away from me with ten feet to spare and dived over the bank down toward the courtyard below. A shadow streaked out of Renaldo's driveway and ran up the road away from me. I took off after him, but he was leaving me in his dust.

Thirty feet ahead of him light was spilling out of a window and across the road. I stopped, and when he ran through the light, I shot him in the thigh. I didn't aim for the center and the bone because shattering that much bone just might have killed him, but the bullet ripped through enough muscle to send him spinning and sprawling into the road. I was on him before he stopped rolling, just in case he had a gun. If he'd been counting, he'd know that my gun was empty.

I frisked him, fast and rough, and didn't find anything on him at all. He wasn't even carrying a wallet or a pack of cigarettes. He whimpered and scrunched into a one-legged fetal position to hug his injured leg. I grabbed his other foot and sledded him down the road on his back. Renaldo met me at the driveway, and together we bumped the guy right up the stairs and into the house.

Everything was quiet, but I was eager to get inside

because I felt naked out there with an empty gun. We dumped the bundle just inside the door. I raced up the stairs, ejected the casings into the sock drawer, and reloaded. I grabbed a few more shells and shoved them into my pocket, the way I should have in the first place.

I bounded back downstairs and through Renaldo's room to duck out the window again. The lawn was bare. I crawled to the end of the hedge and surveyed the road. The streetlight made a bright pool at the corner and a murky twilight that reached most of the way up to Renaldo's yard. If anything had moved on the road, it would have been visible.

I could hear a lot of commotion going on below the road, but I couldn't see down into the courtyard. A cop car wheeled into a driveway on the next street down, and a minute later an ambulance showed up. Two guys jumped out of the ambulance and carried a stretcher toward the hill, out of my range of vision.

When they came back, they didn't seem to be in a hurry. They dumped the contents of the stretcher on the floor of their van, and wandered back for two more loads. They drove away without sirens or flashers, so apparently no one from the car was expected to live. Renaldo's porch and front door appeared entirely too well lighted for my taste. I crawled back along the hedge and climbed in through the bedroom window.

Renaldo had the new guest stretched out on the carpet with a plastic tablecloth under him and a tourniquet on his leg. The guest was a reasonable facsimile of the sniper from the domino building, but this one was dressed all in black except for a pair of Nike running shoes. This one wasn't the silent type. Judging by the staccato cadence, he was hollering a stream of invectives. Renaldo didn't seem to be getting them, so maybe they were in Portuguese again.

"I don't suppose he gave you his name, rank, and serial number?" I asked.

"I don't know what he gave me, except a hard time. I don't think he likes me very much."

"Do you think Juan would like to come down again and interrogate him?" I asked.

A voice behind us said, "That won't be necessary." Renaldo and I both spun toward the hallway, and there stood Paloma, wearing a short wine-colored robe, with a net over her hair.

"Hey, you speak English." I was shocked, but I'd never thought to ask.

"Yes, I've spoken English all my life. Mama was a gringa; I guess that's why they sent me to UCLA."

"And you speak Portuguese?" Renaldo was looking at my girl with a whole new interest.

"That's my first language. I'm from Brazil."

"So, you know what this guy is saying?" I prompted.

"Yes, I know, but I wouldn't repeat it. It wouldn't help you much anyhow, but it doesn't matter. I know this guy."

"What?" Renaldo and I spoke together that time.

"He works for my Uncle Dominic. I think there might be a bomb in your car. That's the sort of trick this weasel is good at."

"Can you give us a hint about why?" I asked.

"Well, I know why it would normally be, but I thought you guys were gold miners. Uncle Dom runs a cocaine cartel, so bombing cars is usually just competition." Paloma came over to inspect our new prisoner. She said something like, "Hola, Paco", and gave him a barefoot kick on his bad leg. He screamed, and she bent over him to spit in his face. I got the impression they were not old friends.

Renaldo scooped the dregs of our drinks off the coffee table and carried them into the kitchen. The ice had melted, and the glasses looked a little scuzzy. He came back with fresh drinks in fresh tumblers and a glass of white wine for Paloma. He set them on the dining table and the three of us sat down for a war council.

"Why the hell should a cocaine cartel be bothering us?" Renaldo wondered.

"Renaldo," I explained, "I've been hinting at this for a while, but in plain English, your gold mine is as queer as a three-dollar bill with the picture of the wrong president on it."

"How can that be? We ship out the gold. I sign the bills of lading myself... "

"Renaldo, you ship out a product. Cocaine shipments aren't usually registered. They're called coffee, or sweet potatoes, or anything else except what they are. You, my sweet innocent friend, are the gringo front man for a major drug smuggling operation."

Paloma nodded. "That makes sense. When I heard the shooting, and then Paco swearing out here, I thought they had come for me."

"Why you?" I asked.

"Uncle Dom got the idea that my parents were cooperating with the American DEA. Maybe they were. Mama wasn't happy about the business. Anyway, he had our house bombed, and Paco over there was probably the one who did it. I was late getting home that night, and when I got there our house was just gone, and my family with it. I've been hiding out for the last six months."

"Maybe we should call the police?" I suggested.

Paloma giggled at that. Maybe it was because she had finished her wine, but her giggle seemed to have an edge of hysteria to it. Renaldo ran to pour her another glass.

"Whether you should call the police or not depends on who they belong to. If they belong to Uncle Dom, and they find you've shot one of his soldiers, the police will just finish his job for him."

Renaldo was frowning, but not necessarily disagreeing. "The police picked up a dead sniper last week and they didn't seem to mind."

Paloma took that as good news. "Well then, that tells you who they belong to."

"So, maybe we should call them for Paco? He needs medical attention." I looked over at the body on the floor, and he was looking pretty pale, barely breathing. "We'd better do something pretty soon. He's in shock."

Paloma gave a dismissive shrug, and Renaldo made the call. The same lieutenant showed up and nodded with approval at the drape over the window. He was accompanied by two ex-football linebackers, or maybe they were rugby players since we were in Venezuela. The two officers grabbed Paco by the arms and stood him up, but he just slumped between them. They carried him outside with his toes dragging. The lieutenant stepped outside, and we heard a shot. I grabbed my gun and dived out the door onto the porch floor, expecting to see dead policemen.

The lieutenant was calmly holstering his smoking gun. Paco had a new hole in his back, and his escorts were dragging him right along. The lieutenant gave me a shrug.

"He tried to escape," the lieutenant explained.

Chapter 12

"Jeez, Alex, I can't just go to work like nothing has happened."

"You damn well better and you'd better be the most innocent gold miner in Venezuela. I don't think Julio will take it well if you accuse him of dealing in drugs."

Renaldo was dressed for work, sharp tan suit and red tie, but he was pacing like a caged polar bear. "Maybe we should head for the airport and grab the first flight to Tasmania or Borneo."

"I don't think that's such a good idea, either. If Julio owns the police, he probably owns some customs officials, too, and he won't much like it if you try to skip out. So long as you're a good little accountant and keep signing all the incriminating paperwork yourself, you're perfectly safe. It's Paloma I'm worried about."

"Why Paloma? She can just go back to her nest on the

hill." Renaldo ran his hands through his hair, a gesture I hadn't seen since finals week in college.

I went to pour two more cups of coffee, and shoved Renaldo down into a chair at the table. He needed to do some serious calming down, but everything I was thinking was only going to agitate him more.

"Paloma could have stayed in her nest if I'd left her alone, but I brought her down here. Now her uncle may know where she is. If he knows she's here, he'll think she joined your drug cartel."

"Don't call it *my* drug cartel."

"Okay, Julio's cartel, whatever. I think Uncle Dom has decided to branch out and take over this territory, and that means we're in the middle of a war. Speaking of wars, we'd better check out your car before you take off. There just might be a bomb in it."

We sipped coffee for a while. Neither of us wanted to open the front door. Finally I went over and peeked out the window behind the drape. It was a typically peaceful, sunny morning outside. No new windows were open in the sniper's building, and no gun barrels were sticking out of the broken one. I opened the drapes and the sunshine took a little of the menace out of the air. Renaldo came over to look, and I noticed him pat the automatic in his pocket.

"Hey, you can't take that in to work with you."

"I'm not stepping out that door without it."

"Okay, but leave it in the car when you park. Once you're inside the parking garage, you'll be covered by enough guns for a revolution. Julio will like it better if all the guns belong to him. Speaking of revolutions, you'd better tell Julio about last night. The cops will have already told him anyway, and it won't hurt if you pretend to be a little scared. Just stay utterly mystified about the reason."

"Okay, I guess I can pretend to be a little scared."

Renaldo opened the door and politely gestured for me to go first. We marched across the porch double time, trying not to hunker down. The Jaguar's hood was still up. A wire was stuffed up under the rubber cap on the ignition coil, and another was wrapped around the ground terminal on the battery, but both wires ended in terminal lugs. The bomb was a brown plastic package still sitting on the ground beside the car. I picked it up. It weighed two pounds, and it wasn't ticking.

"Hey, don't touch that thing. Let's call the police." Renaldo shied away.

"It's okay. Paco was doing a nice professional job here. This was meant to be set off by an electrical arc, so that's what it would take. In the meantime, we might find a use for it. Bombs sometimes come in handy in wars." I jerked the wires out of the car and wrapped them around the bomb. Just for good measure, I dropped down and looked underneath the car, but the dirt was undisturbed.

"Have a good day at the office," I suggested.

Renaldo grimaced, but he climbed in and started the car. It did not explode. He drove away down the hill, and I carried the bomb upstairs and stashed it in the sock drawer.

It was time for me to take a walk. I don't know why, but if I sit and try to think, nothing much happens. If I go for a walk and check out a new scene, my mind usually wanders off to where the problem is.

I stuck the gun in my belt, covered it with my windbreaker, and for a change took off up the road away from the stairway. The road topped a rise, ducked down for half a block and ended in a circle big enough to turn a small car around. A house hung over the road on the uphill side, with a new Buick parked under it. Straight ahead an empty driveway, one car-length long, flanked another wooden house. On the downhill side, a wooden stairway led down to the next street across from the park. I tromped down the stairs.

The park looked like a high school commons at lunchtime. Several teenagers were milling around in groups under banyan trees. No one was sitting on the golf-course-grade lawn or paying any attention to the hibiscus and bougainvillea. The boys all wore white shirts and black slacks, the girls, white blouses and dark skirts. They were keeping an eye on the theater across the street, waiting for the doors to open.

The marquee was in Spanish and didn't tell me much, but the front of the theater was plastered with pictures that reminded me of Errol Flynn swinging through the rigging of a pirate ship. He was holding the swing rope and a cutlass in the same hand because he had a well-endowed lass in a torn blouse under his other arm.

The group of students had an almost military ambiance. They were happy, and even nodded to me in a friendly manner, but they were all super clean. Haircuts and shoe shines struck me as regulation, and no horseplay was going on.

I passed the park and circled down between houses, lawns, and shrubs, toward the waterfront. It seemed to me that Renaldo was in serious danger, regardless of the outcome of this particular war. To Uncle Dom, he was just part of the enemy to be eliminated. To Julio he was an expendable cover. Any paper trails that the DEA or the ATF, or IRS, or any other acronym might follow would lead straight to Renaldo. If Julio felt a need to cover tracks, all he had to do was expunge Renaldo. Uncle Dom's stirring the pot might lead Julio in that direction.

My street ended at the four-lane boulevard along the water, and I turned left toward town. The edge of the boulevard was a low cement railing with boulders down to the water. Several old men were fishing, tending poles propped in the rocks. La Guaira has a good-sized harbor, ruffled to a chop by the breeze, and smelling like Seattle or Boston.

I thought about all the movies that feature drug cartel wars and it struck me there were quite a few. Most of the plots concluded with massive explosions, but the tactics along the way included destroying each other's shipments and enlisting various agencies. I wished to heck this were a movie, but the waterfront breeze and the screaming seagulls were stark reality.

The docks were coming up on the right, with Renaldo's building a block ahead, when gunfire erupted. It sounded like one of those Chinese New Year's firecracker strings. The windows to Renaldo's offices were exploding and raining glass down on the sidewalk. I thought at first that the shots were coming from inside, but the guns sounded too loud. The shots were coming from three sedans parked on the street in the next block.

The shooting stopped, the three sedans peeled out into the street and screeched toward me. I jerked the .357 out of my belt and jumped over the little cement guardrail beside the sidewalk. The sedans raced my way, and I put a bullet in the front tire of each one as they passed. The first driver recovered from his skid and went lumping and weaving on down the street, but the second one skidded broadside and the third plowed into him.

Three men jumped out of each car, a driver and two shooters. The shooters were each carrying automatic rifles. One of the gunmen spotted me and raised his rifle. I nailed him between the eyes, but two more saw me shoot.

If you've ever walked down Broadway at noon stark naked, then you know how I felt. I dived down between the rocks behind me, and wriggled toward the water like a seal off an ice flow when a polar bear climbs on. Barnacles and mussels on the rocks were ripping at my shirt and going deeper, like a cheese grater through cheddar, but at the moment I didn't mind losing a little skin, so long as it was the outside layer.

The last rock between me and the water was the size of a Volkswagon bug laying sideways and I dived over it. The next rock was under only two inches of water, so my dive ended in a crunching belly flop. I felt my left arm jam up into my shoulder, and ribs crack. Bullets and rock chips whined everywhere. I tried to crawl, but it hurt my ribs too much. I rolled over far enough to poke my head and the gun around the end of the rock.

Four or five guys were leaning over the railing with weapons, waiting for me to surface thirty feet out, which I would have done if my dive had been better. I shot two of them, jammed my gun into my belt, and slid backward into the water. I wished again I was in one of those movies so I could have shot the rest of them, but in real life, six shots is all you get from a revolver.

I didn't try to swim away. My ribs hurt so bad that a deep breath was out, and my left arm didn't seem to be working very well. I pulled myself along the edge of the rocks toward the first dock, and wondered why the shooters hadn't come down after me, until I heard the police sirens. I heard a heck of a lot more shooting, but it wasn't coming my way. I just kept scrabbling toward the docks in case the wrong side won the battle.

By the time I reached the first dock, I could still hear sirens but no more shots. I pulled myself under the dock and squeezed past a rusty metal fishing boat hull. After I passed the dock, I didn't feel so naked anymore. I found a solid rock that wasn't too high out of the water, and tried to climb up. A hand came down to help me.

It was a big brown hand with a gold-and-jade fraternity ring, sticking out of a virgin white cuff with gold links, and that came out of a tropical tan suit coat. I didn't need to see the face to know it was Renaldo.

"Hi, Alex. I thought you'd be around here. That mess down the street looks like your sort of booboo."

"Hey, ouch, easy does it. Right hand only, slow and steady."

Renaldo's sunny smile clouded over. "Are you shot?"

"I don't think so. I just made a bad dive." Renaldo hauled me up. My shirt was in tatters with all the buttons ripped off. Renaldo opened the flaps to survey the damage. Quite a lot of blood was oozing around, and things were turning blue and purple.

"Good Lord, did you dive off the top of a building?"

"No, it wasn't exactly a high dive. I just missed the ocean."

"Seems like I've warned you about that. I think my immortal words used to be 'look before you leap.' Come on over to the officc. A whole team of doctors is over there picking glass out of people. Maybe one of them can find time to tape you up. I don't suppose you brought any dry clothes with you?"

"Sorry, I packed in a hurry."

"Well, try not to drip on the carpets, particularly blood." He walked, I sloshed, across the street. Two guards stood beside the door with automatic rifles in their hands, but they nodded to Renaldo and we entered the lobby. Another guard looked us over and punched the elevator button. When we stepped through the office door on the fifth floor, I beeped. A seven-foot-tall, three-hundred-pound guard grabbed me from behind, and a .45 automatic that looked as big as a twelve gauge was suddenly jabbed into my jugular vein. The man-mountain jerked my .357 out of my belt and shoved me into the room.

The office looked like the aftermath of a blizzard. Everything was covered with white plaster dust, and the air was still full of it, so it was foggy inside. Doors to Julio's office and Renaldo's office stood open. The ceilings were stitched and pocked with holes from bullets that had been going up. Thousands of glass shards were scattered everywhere, reflecting sunlight from the naked windows.

Julio was leaning against a desk in the reception area, and a doctor was stitching up his arm with a needle and thread. Julio shoved the doctor away and came over with his hand out. He nodded at the granite pillar of a man I'd been leaning against. The pillar released me, the .45 disappeared, and he handed my revolver to Julio. Julio swung the cylinder and dumped the empty shells into his hand. He handed the pistol back to me.

Julio had a thread sticking out of a gash in his arm with a needle dangling from it. We walked back over to the white-jacketed doctor. The doctor caught the needle and continued sewing up Julio.

"You're pretty good with that thing." Julio nodded toward the pistol. He was in a jovial mood for a guy who had just had the arm cut off a two-thousand-dollar suit, his pants soaked in blood, and some kid in a white coat and granny glasses making hem stitches down his arm.

I must have looked quizzical because he continued. "I watched you from the window. Six shots, three tires and three stooges. How many bullets do we need to dig out of you?" Julio was looking at my shirt, and I was dripping blood on his carpet in spite of Renaldo's injunction. I was a little ashamed to admit that all I needed was some ribs taped, and maybe a sling for my left arm.

Another medic, in a white coat with serious bloodstains, came over carrying a bag, which he plunked down on the desk next to the sewing kit. He grabbed my shirt from behind and started to rip it off so I unbuttoned the sleeves and let it go. He pulled a wad of cotton out of his bag, doused it in alcohol from a white plastic bottle and took a swipe at the blood on my chest.

I didn't scream outwardly, but you should have heard me on the inside. I thought I knew about pain. One time I mashed my big toe when a float dock slipped out of a hoisting sling. I spent forty-eight hours sitting in a chair rubbing ice cubes on my toe and trying not to scream, but by comparison that was nothing. Alcohol in the scrapes on my chest must have been what it was like to be burned at the stake.

I leaned back against the desk next to Julio and tried to crush the wooden edge of the desk by squeezing. Julio was watching my alcohol bath with the same detachment that he had been watching the kid stitch up his arm. I managed a silent stoic outside, but my inside was seething. "The Lord is my shepherd, I shall not want... yeow!" The guy with the swab was zeroing in on the source of the blood. It was coming from my shoulder, two inches from my neck.

My left arm was numb, so when Torquemada started digging around in the hole in my shoulder, it really didn't hurt too badly. He used a pair of tweezers to pull some white slivers out of the hole and stuffed in a wad of gauze. The blood stopped running down my front. He grabbed my arm and pulled me around. This guy really needed some work on his bedside, or desk-side, manner. He started washing my back.

Renaldo was watching the show and making grimaces that waggled his mustache at crazy angles. The medic took a swipe up my back that felt cool and tingly, and then poured a slug of liquid fire into my shoulder.

"What the hell is he doing back there?" I managed to grunt between clenched teeth.

"Bullet hole." Renaldo seemed to think it was kind of neat. He picked up the white slivers off the desk to show me.

"Looks like it went right through. These are slivers off your collar bone." He held up what looked like a couple of broken and well-chewed tooth picks.

The medic ran a hot poker or some diabolically more painful modern equivalent of one, through the hole in my shoulder and stuck on some bandages here and there. The kid working on Julio's arm came to the end of the cut just above the elbow and tied off his thread.

All that Glisters // 123

"Renaldo," Julio interrupted Renaldo's inspection. "There's a bottle of brandy and some glasses in the bottom left-hand drawer of my desk."

"Good idea. I'm feeling a little sick." Renaldo tromped through the glass and plaster and came back with a bottle of Courvosier and three glasses. The medics wandered off in search of more victims. Julio held his left arm straight and stiff, but he took the bottle in his left hand to remove the cap, and transferred it to his right hand to pour into the three glasses Renaldo had lined up on the desk.

We each grabbed a snifter, toasted each other silently, and downed the brandy as if it was water. The fire on the inside sort of balanced the fire on the outside, and felt pretty good. I noticed that most of the flames on my chest had gone out. Only a couple of coals were winking on and off at the deepest scrapes. We plunked our glasses down on the desk, and Julio refilled them.

Renaldo noticed some plaster dust on his fingers. He pulled a handkerchief from his breast pocket and carefully wiped his fingers clean before he picked up his snifter again.

"You seem to have survived the attack pretty well." I gave him a quizzical glance and took a more dignified sip of the brandy.

"I heard all hell break loose in Julio's office, so I came running. I was out here when my office exploded. These shoes are ruined though." Renaldo lifted one foot to demonstrate a cut across the toe of one highly-polished oxford.

"Tough luck," I commiserated.

"Shall we run home and change?" Renaldo suggested. "You could really use a fresh shirt."

"Not right now. The three of us need to have a serious

talk." I turned to Julio. "Where are your other two partners?"

"What other partners?" Julio tried to pin me to the wall with his stare again, but between the pain and the brandy, it didn't work.

"Julio, it's time to cut the crap. We're not playing games here. Two of your partners are dead, you two are lucky not to be, and one of your partners is a traitor."

Julio winced for the first time. I'd hurt him a lot worse than the gash on his arm had. He'd been unbending a little with the camaraderie of the carnage, but I watched him turn to stone again.

"Go on," he said. "And this had better be good."

I sat down on the desk. My left arm was hanging limp and funny, so I stuck my hand in my belt Napoleon fashion.

"Okay," I said, "you just made my point for me. You keep your operation so secretive that I'm not even supposed to know there were six partners. I don't see any signs around, so how did the shooters know which windows to shoot? How many people know where Renaldo lives, or even that he works here? Who knew that Zeke was a partner and where he lived? Who knew that Joseph was going to drive to the mine, and what happened to his air conditioning?"

I stopped for more brandy. I had Julio's attention all right. I looked at the muscles about to pop out of his jaw and decided to go for broke. The office boy with the bulges was missing, so just for that moment Renaldo and I had Julio outnumbered.

"Another thing. It's time to drop the bullshit about the gold mine. Change the mercury shipments to coca leaves, or whatever you make the white powder out of, and at least all of this makes some sense. It's up to us three to keep each other alive, and we'll do a lot better if we're honest with each other."

If Julio had had a gun in his hand, he would have shot me, but I was pretty sure his gun was in his desk drawer. During our first meeting, when he was deciding whether to shoot me or not, his right hand had kept trying to reach for his upper right-hand desk drawer and he kept pulling it back.

Julio was thinking, but he glanced through the open door to the desk in his office. I slid off my perch and walked into his office. I pulled the Luger out of his desk drawer and brought it back to the reception desk cum wet bar. When you're bluffing in a poker game and your opponents are getting suspicious, your best strategy is to make a bid so outrageous that no one will believe it. They'll decide you were sucking them in by pretending to bluff. That's what I did to Julio. I carried his gun out to him and laid it on the desk beside his brandy snifter.

For a few seconds there, Renaldo forgot his appearance and stood with his mouth hanging open. The ends of his mustache seemed to droop. Julio looked down at the Luger for a long time, then he grunted, shoved it away with the back of his hand and picked up the brandy bottle. I extended a half-empty snifter, and he topped it off and refilled his own. Renaldo drained his glass and held it out for a refill.

Chapter 13

We left the Jag in the parking garage and walked the block to the Hotel Venezuelan. Renaldo magnanimously let me wear his suit coat, but he sort of cringed along the street, ashamed to be seen in his shirtsleeves. We rented a three-bedroom suite on the top floor. The clerk looked a little dubious at our appearance, but Renaldo pulled out one of the banded bundles of U.S. hundreds he'd brought from the office safe.

That's not my field of expertise, but I guessed the packets were ten thousand dollars each. Renaldo wet his finger and flipped out twenty bills like a card shark with a deck. The deck in his hand wasn't noticeably reduced, and the clerk shoved the register at him to sign.

"If you're going to be John Smith again, I want to be John Doe." I goaded him. Renaldo scribbled two names. "Don't forget Paloma-Jane Doe." He scribbled one more name and took three keys from the clerk. An attendant pushed the elevator button for us and was looking for luggage. Renaldo handed him a bill, not one of the hundreds, and waved him away.

During the ride up to the 36th floor, I couldn't help wriggling my good shoulder to make the jacket sway. Renaldo had loaded it up with bundles of money before he loaned it to me, so all those bulging pockets felt pretty good. I may have had that much money on my person once before. I went to Chicago one time to pick up a new helicopter for Bushmaster and paid two-hundred thousand for it on the spot, but that was a cashier's check, and it didn't have the hedonistic feel of the jacket full of cash.

We weren't stealing the company money. Renaldo was always in charge of the cash, and since we were vacating the offices for renovation, he emptied the safe on general principles. When I had asked Julio whether the name Dominic meant anything to him, he turned a kind of swarthy pale. He gave a whistle. Guards appeared from everywhere, some bandaged and dusty, some from the hall still clean. So much for Renaldo and me outnumbering him.

Julio and the guards charged out the door, Julio leading the way with his Luger, leaving Renaldo and me to clean up. The medics seemed to have left. Renaldo cleared out the safe, stuffing money in pockets, and then filling a shopping bag. He would have packed up the contents of his desk if I hadn't screamed at him that we had to leave. I also nixed the idea of going back to the house for clothes.

"The surgical strikes are over," I pointed out. "It's blitzkrieg time now. The only reason you guys survived was that the angle was bad. The shots were going up so all they hit was the ceiling. When they pull the same trick on the house, we won't be so lucky."

The hotel had four suites on the 36th floor, and the keys in Renaldo's hand said PH 2. That was the penthouse on the ocean-sunset corner. The suite wasn't overly posh, but it was clean and comfortable, about like a Howard Johnson's or a Best Western. I handed Renaldo's jacket to him, and he dumped the bundles of cash into a desk drawer. He emptied out his pants pockets, and I handed him the overflow from mine. He stuck the shopping bag in on top of the bundles.

He took the jacket into a bathroom next to the living room and inspected it for blood. He dusted it off with a towel and got back into uniform. I turned into the first bedroom on the right. I wasn't bleeding anymore, but just to be safe, I grabbed a towel from the bathroom and spread it on the bed before I crashed.

Renaldo had some errands to run, like paying Maria a month in advance and telling her to stay home, advising Paloma of her new address and forbidding her to go near the house, and buying some clothes for all of us. What I had to do was take a nap. I handled my part with efficiency and dispatch.

It might have been Renaldo and Paloma who woke me. They were talking softly in the living room. My head and eyes had that dull feeling you get when you've been sleeping too hard, but I didn't seem to have any fever. Torquemada may have gotten his jollies by inflicting pain, but apparently he had cleaned things up all right, so no infection.

Seawater was considered a disinfectant when I was growing up, but I think that time is gone. I wouldn't say that La Guaira was dumping raw effluent into the bay, but

I hadn't noticed any sewage treatment plants anywhere. I didn't hurt until I moved, and even then the pains were dull like a bass fiddle, instead of the piccolo and cymbals I went to sleep with.

A new shirt was laid out on the bed, so I slipped it on. At first I thought Renaldo had bought a size too large, but with the bandages it fit fine. Nice threads. I should have Renaldo buy all my clothes. I snapped off the light in the bedroom and went looking for the crowd.

The living room was dark except for two candles on a dining table at the far end of the room. Two walls of the suite were glass, with moonlit ocean on the left and the moon itself over the mountains on the right. Streetlights and traffic below looked picturesque and innocuous. I couldn't see Renaldo's house or the domino building because they were on the other side of the hotel, but maybe that was a good thing.

Renaldo and Paloma sat by the candles, digging into Crab Louis from room service. Mine was sitting on the table and covered by Saran wrap. The table was meant to seat six with two on each side and one at each end. Renaldo had the head of the table with Paloma on his left, so I took the chair across from her on Renaldo's right. Renaldo pulled a bottle of Chenin Blanc out of an ice bucket and poured for me.

I speared a big chunk of crab leg off my pile and dabbed just a smear of the Louis dressing on it. It was cool and juicy, with all the flavor and subtle overtones of a well-fed Dungeness. I had to close my eyes to savor that morsel. At that moment, I knew why people fight so hard to stay alive. It's so they can have more Crab Louis from a good kitchen in a nice hotel in Venezuela.

"You okay?" Renaldo asked.

I chewed pure heaven until it was gone and opened my eyes. There sat Paloma, candle light glistening on her hair and building dancing fires in her eyes. She glowed with the softness and perfection that only happens to beautiful women in candlelight, and her mouth was pursed with what I took to be concern for me.

"Yeah, old buddy, I'm fine. In fact, I can't remember ever being better." I dragged my eyes off Paloma to spear another chunk of crab. Paloma gave me that original smile that had left me paralyzed on the mountain, and attacked her own Louis. I was fine, too. My table manners had improved. I was sitting nice and straight with my left hand resting in my lap, just the way it's supposed to. I had never really mastered that trick before.

"I was just telling Paloma how you accused Julio of drug trafficking, then handed him a gun and stared him down until he decided not to shoot us."

"Au contraire. What Julio decided was not to shoot us right at that moment. He probably figured he didn't have time right then to unscramble the mess you've undoubtedly made of his bookkeeping. He decided to shoot us, but later. He's probably already called a temp service for your replacement."

"Renaldo thinks that Julio went after Uncle Dom." Paloma blotted her lips with her napkin and took a sip of her wine. The way her glass compressed her lip, the soft muscles of her throat working in the candlelight, a man could go insane with speculation. Heck of a lot safer to think about Julio and Uncle Dom shooting each other.

"I think that's a fair assumption. How do you rate his chances?"

All that Glisters // 131

Paloma frowned and speared a slice of boiled egg, but tantalized it by not letting it touch her lips yet. "If Julio is lucky enough even to find Uncle Dom, then he must have won a major lottery every day of his life." She took pity on the egg and popped it in.

Renaldo was rolling the stem of his wine glass between his fingers. "So, if a war is in progress, just which side are we on?"

I tried Paloma's trick with the napkin. "The way I see it, we have an eternal triangle here. Uncle Dom will have us shot on sight. Julio will have us shot when it suits him. I think we're on our own side, and maybe just a little disadvantaged in the war department."

"Why not just run?" Renaldo asked. "If we can't go out through customs, we could steal an airplane, or even buy one, and you could fly us out of here."

"Well, that's a plan, but it isn't Plan A or B. That's about Plan F, and here's why." I sat back, glass in hand, and tried to look erudite. "When a rich and powerful man wants you dead, running is a temporary solution. You mentioned that the jeweler in Miami has contacts all over the country. Every one of those contacts is salivating to do a favor for Julio. You know how well the Federal Witness Protection Program works? About like those helicopters that were built in 1910."

"So, what is Plan A?" Paloma seemed to be buying my erudition act.

"Well, that's the catch, Paloma. I haven't the foggiest, but for starters, you have to stop going to work every day."

"Why does that matter?" Lovely pout. Oh those lips.

"It matters, my dear, because you're just too damn beautiful. You're such a classy chick that every man you pass is going to watch you and remember where you went."

"Been kissing the Blarney stone?" She tried to look scornful, but she wasn't minding a bit.

"Not at all. Look what happened to me, and I'm no more vulnerable than the average shmuk on the street. I saw you for ten seconds on the mountain, followed you all the way to town, couldn't get you out of my mind for a week, and finally went after you."

Renaldo gave me a "go for it" nudge under the table with his knee. I wondered if he realized I'd learned the technique from him.

"Another thing," seems like I never quit when I'm ahead, "you tried running from Uncle Dom. You ran until you came to the ocean, then climbed so far up a mountain that no one would ever find you, and lived like a monk in Shangri La. I came along, all innocent and good intentioned, and dumped you right back in Uncle Dom's lap."

"So, you're saying we have to stay here and fight?" Renaldo shared the last of the wine, pouring about six drops into each of our glasses and jamming the bottle back in the ice upside down.

"Well, that's how it seems to me. In a kind of a way, both Uncle Dom and Julio are on our side at the moment. Maybe there'll be a Shakespearian ending. Maybe everyone will kill everyone in Act Three. We need to get rid of Paloma though. She's too visible and too memorable. Why don't you take her up to Caracas and stick her into that hotel of yours until this is over?"

"Not on your life, Buster." Paloma slammed her empty wine glass down on the table. "Your Irish Blarney bullshit is just fine, you silver-tongued bastard. It's even working, but right now I'm one of the Three Musketeers. For one thing,

I'll be a big help flushing out Uncle Dom. You Romeos wouldn't know him if you met him on the street."

Paloma jumped up and stomped off to the middle bedroom. She very nearly slammed the door that time.

"Did you buy any rum?" I asked.

"Do boys and girls play doctor?" Renaldo went to the refrigerator and came back with the balm of Gilead.

"Did you remember the ammunition?"

"One box each, .357 and .25, except my Beretta is in the car in the parking garage. Shall I go back for it?"

"I wouldn't go back to that building right now if you had left a howitzer there."

Chapter 14

Well, we did go back to Caracas, but Paloma had made it pretty clear we weren't leaving her there. Good old ubiquitous Hertz brought a Chrysler New Yorker around to the hotel. I rented it in my name. Julio might remember the Alex, but I doubt he'd know the Price part.

The New Yorker was wide enough for the three of us to sit in front. Renaldo drove, out of deference to my injured wing, and Paloma sat between us. Just to make more room, I laid my left arm across the seat behind Paloma. I could leave it there for about ten minutes, then put it back in my lap, but it was probably good exercise.

We checked into the El Conde in three separate rooms, but they were adjoining, with connecting doors between them. Paloma took the center one. We freshened up and met in the bar. Booze hound that I am, I was the first one down. I wasn't going to admit it, but just between us, my arm was aching a bit and I was looking for some painkiller. The Chrysler was smooth as silk, and the highway was good, but the arm was still protesting too much movement.

I stopped at the bar and ordered my dark Myers and Coke. Paloma came in and ordered sweet vermouth. We carried our drinks to a corner table. Renaldo came in bouncing and beaming.

"Hey, Benny, how ya been? I came back for one of your famous Hurricanes." Benny mixed and dashed, and almost beat Renaldo to our table.

"Do you really think you should fly with that crippled wing?" Renaldo asked. He scooted his chair up, clapped Benny on the back, and accepted his Hurricane.

"Won't be a problem," I assured him, and hoped it was true. "We'll rent something small and light, I'll give you a couple of lessons as we go along, and we'll do fine."

"Is this a sexist conversation?" Paloma asked. "Why not teach me?"

"Nothing sexist about it. It's just that sometimes it helps to swear at students, and I'll be more comfortable swearing at Renaldo."

We stayed in the bar, ate braised sirloin tips over noodles, and tried to exhaust Benny's inexhaustible supply. By the time we were propping each other up in the elevator for the ride to the 6th floor, I was feeling no pain, almost.

I tried lying on my front, but that didn't work very well. I tried lying on my back. That was worse. I had just tried the front again, this time with a pillow under my chest so my shoulder hung down, when the door from Paloma's room opened quietly. She tiptoed over to check if I was sleeping. She was wearing a short blue nightgown, what I think might be called a baby doll, and was carrying a glass in her hand.

"Hi," she whispered. She sat on the edge of the bed. "I brought you something you might need."

That set my imagination to dancing. The silhouette of Paloma sitting there in her nightgown was something I'd been needing all my life. She set the glass on the nightstand. She checked my forehead for fever with a soft cool palm, and then bent to give me a peck on my fevered brow. It hadn't been fevered when she came in, but it was getting that way fast. She slipped away and closed her door again. I didn't hear it lock, but I definitely heard it click shut.

I checked the nightstand. She had brought me a glass of water and two Advil tablets. Her judgment was pretty good. I popped the pills, drank half the water, and slept as if I'd been innocent.

We met for a late breakfast in the coffee shop. There wasn't any banter. We were each dealing with our own hangovers in our own way. A pot of coffee, pitchers of orange juice, and plates of toast with poached eggs made life seem livable again.

Paloma and I held up a pillar in the loading area while Renaldo congratulated the bellman over Conchita's recovery and the lot boy brought the car around. Renaldo threaded the Chrysler through the gauntlet of the Autopista Del Este to the municipal Aeropuerto De Carlotta.

The twenty-year-old kid at the flight school was dressed like an airline captain in blue slacks and shirt with chevrons, but no tie. His black hair was slicked back formally, and the kid could have passed for a flight instructor, but he was absorbed in reading *Flying Magazine* in Spanish, and couldn't be bothered with us. He glanced at my license and my medical certificate, pointed at a Piper Tri-pacer that was emanating heat waves in the lot, and went back to reading.

Tri-pacers are not my favorite airplanes, but that's because the cowling is high and the windshield is slanted so far forward you can't reach it. That can be a problem if the windshield is frosting over, but that didn't appear likely at the moment. It was over 80 degrees and clear, except the sky was more brown than blue, thanks to several million cars and buses.

The best thing about the Tri-pacer is it's built like the little teapot, "short and stout." It has a good solid feel in turbulence. The Cessna equivalent would be the 172, which has a much longer, narrower wing. In severe turbulence, like you're apt to get in Alaska's Windy Pass on the north side of Mt. Denali, the Cessna wings will flap like a bird. The Piper just slams up and down like you'd expect a brick outhouse to feel, if you happened to be flying one.

I checked the plane over pretty closely in case the mechanic was as lackadaisical as the instructor, but it seemed okay. The fuel tanks were full, the oil dip stick showed six quarts, and it was dirty. I liked that. If the oil is too clean, the engine has either just been worked on, or burns oil so fast it never has a chance to get dirty.

Paloma gave me a look and climbed in back. I took the left seat, Renaldo buckled himself in on the right. The engine cranked for a good long time and took several shots of primer before it started, but once it fired, it sounded smooth. The engine just hadn't been run for a while. I tried a magneto check, and the engine darn near stopped when I switched to the right magneto only. I pulled the mixture control a little too lean to heat things up and burn off the soot. I tried it again, and it was okay. That airplane just needed to have the cobwebs blown out.

I ran down the frequency list and called ground control for permission to taxi. The response that came out of the speakers bore no resemblance to any words I had ever heard.

"What did he say? What did he say?" I asked Renaldo.

"Darned if I know. What was he supposed to say?"

"He said, 'Taxi to runway two-four'," Paloma translated from the back seat, so I turned left and followed the signs.

That traffic controller was not speaking some foreign language. All aviation communications worldwide are in English, at least theoretically. It's a given, like red means stop, and green means go. It's a matter of international convention. However, one of the flying stories that always gives me goose bumps comes from my old buddy Walt who runs the charter service at McGrath, Alaska.

Walt took off from Poland one dark and stormy night, flew clear across Germany on instruments, and never understood a word that a traffic controller said to him until he was over France. If that story doesn't give you goose bumps, it's because you don't realize that some of the communiqués could have been routing him around a collision course with a 747.

"Taxi into position and hold," Paloma translated. "If we're six-three-nine-seven-one, then we're cleared for take off." I much prefer the North American system of referring to a plane by two numbers and a letter.

We took off. At thirty-five hundred feet above sea level and eighty-five degrees it wasn't much like a takeoff in Bethel, but the Piper accelerated fast on the hot tarmac. When the airspeed indicator read seventy, I eased back the yoke, and we staggered into the air.

Our destination, per Paloma, was just outside the little town of Altagracia, overlooking Lake Maracaibo. By road, you have a choice of routes. You can follow the coast, or cross the Cordillera de Merido at Trujillo and come back along the lake. I would have loved to follow a road if I knew which one to follow, just on the chance of seeing Julio down there rolling along at the head of a column of tanks and Humvees.

From the Aeropuerto De Carlotta, we swung north and then east to follow the Libertador Vargas past Julio's mine, just in case Uncle Dom had come there with his tanks and Humvees. The mine appeared to be deserted, but that didn't mean anything. It had appeared deserted when I was in the jungle forty feet from the fence.

What surprised me was an airstrip carved out of the jungle. It was a dirt strip that looked fifty feet wide and maybe 4,000 feet long, half a mile from the mine, and connected by a lane through the jungle.

"Did you know that airport was there?" I asked Renaldo.

"Well, I told you that sometimes we send the gold out by charter, so I assumed they must land somewhere."

"Well, I assumed you trucked the gold to some nearby airport, like maybe Kennedy or O'Hare. If you had told me there was an airport at the mine, I wouldn't have wasted a week exploring jungle at the bottom of that hellhole."

"Sorry. You didn't ask." Renaldo shrugged.

We headed straight across the mountains. I guess they're hills by Venezuelan standards because that's the beginning of the Andes, which pop up to ten and fifteen thousand feet just a few miles farther west.

We slipped through the mountains at 5,000 feet and

turned west along the narrow strait that separates Lake Maracaibo from the Gulf of Venezuela. We passed a floating drawbridge several miles long that bisected the lake. Paloma pointed out Uncle Dom's fortress. It was a couple of acres of white hacienda perched on the side of a bluff with a view of the lake on the left, the gulf on the right, and the town of Maracaibo across the strait. The spot could have been picked for its grandeur, but it had a lot in common with the sites of medieval castles. If you wanted to visit Uncle Dom, you had best take the road, and that likely in four-wheel drive.

Other options might include rappelling down a 500-foot cliff into his swimming pool after you walked across the mountains, or crawling through the jungle with your nose in the dirt for twenty miles. Forget any ideas about sneaking in with a helicopter. The jungle down there looked as solid and endless as the tundra around Bethel. We didn't see any sign of Julio and the Light Brigade. In fact, Uncle Dom's aerie looked as deserted as Julio's mine.

"Getting any good ideas?" Renaldo asked.

"Just one. Let's go back and talk that one over with your old buddy Benny."

Just because it was too beautiful to miss, we circled on around the coast and watched the stark-white tour ships milling around the emerald Spice Islands. Curacao made a low double hump on the water, and I was disappointed.

"Hey," I accused Renaldo, "I thought an island that made Curacao Liqueur would be a lot more picturesque and jungley. That looks like a desert out there."

"Quite right, my boy," Renaldo condescended. "About the only thing they can grow there is tourist traps in Willemstad. They make liqueur out of their oranges because they're so scabby and awful they can't sell them as fruit."

That's one problem with traveling, you keep finding out things you don't want to know. Caracas appeared fifty miles away as a brown column of smoke in a pale blue sky.

"You're cleared to land," Paloma translated.

We checked out my good idea with Benny the bartender, and he concurred handsomely. With Benny's help, we were able to assess our situation.

"You don't suppose they're both hiding out from each other so nothing is happening?" Paloma had a point there. The hotel bar had more activity than we'd seen in half a day of flying.

"Maybe we should stir things up a bit. Right now, anything we do to either one will be blamed on the other." Renaldo had a good point too.

Not to be left out, I put in my two cents worth. "Well, we do have a bomb." I bit my tongue. Too late I realized that I had just volunteered to crawl through the jungle again.

We cut Benny off, moved into the coffee shop, and ordered steak and eggs with a pot of coffee. It was getting close to five in the afternoon, but we were making a fresh start, so a second breakfast seemed to be in order.

It was just getting dark when we got to La Guaira. We drove past Renaldo's house. It was still standing, and there were no fresh holes in the window, but the drapes were closed.

"Renaldo, didn't we leave those drapes open?"

"Yeah, sure, we checked for snipers before we left. Paloma? You left last."

"Definitely open. When I came out of my room, I wondered if I should go put some clothes on, but I decided no one could see me."

I did wish Paloma wouldn't say things like that.

"Could Maria have come down and closed them?"

"I doubt it." Renaldo shook his head, "I assured her she'd be killed if she even looked at the house."

Venezuela pulled that tropical trick of getting dark fast. The sun drops straight toward the horizon, so dusk to dark can happen in twenty minutes. Renaldo turned the car around, without lights, and drove back toward the house to the top of the rise. The street light came on down at the corner and muddied the darkness on the road. We could see the front of Renaldo's house and the kitchen window, and it certainly appeared to be dark in there.

The .357 and the penlight were in the jockey box. I took one in each hand and set out to seek my fortune. I skirted the patch of light on the road where I had shot Paco, and came to the driveway. The ground continued to slope up past the end of the driveway, so the kitchen window was just over waist high from the outside. I had gone into the house by two different routes before, the front door and Renaldo's bedroom window. The kitchen window seemed an unlikely entry, and besides it was locked from the inside.

I had worn the dark blue windbreaker again for nighttime camouflage, so I slipped it off and draped it over the window. I used the gun butt to break out the glass and jumped back in case someone was inside. No light, no movement, just a general aura of danger. I shook the glass out of the windbreaker and put it back on before I shined the penlight through the window. The kitchen looked normal, and I didn't see any trip wires or laser beams inside the window.

I stepped through the window into the sink, and jumped down onto the floor. It didn't feel like any one else was in the house. People can usually tell when they're sharing a space, and I felt alone. I carried the flashlight away from my body in my left hand in case someone shot at it, and the pistol in my right hand with the hammer back.

The booby trap was behind the front door. It was rigged with two eyebolts in the doorframe and a string across the door, so when the door opened, it would pull the string. The bomb itself looked pretty much like the car bomb except it had a lever and string where the car bomb had two electrical terminals. The string was loose, so it wasn't holding any mechanism at the moment, and it was cotton, not wire, so there was nothing electrical about it.

I cut the string and thought about taking that bomb with me too, but I decided I didn't want anything to do with any mechanical releases, especially if I was going to try to sneak it through the jungle. Renaldo's bedroom window had the same type bomb, rigged the same way. If I'd stepped through that window, my foot would have been on the string halfway to the floor. I cut that string, too, but left the bomb sitting on Renaldo's bed.

I switched off the penlight, and let my eyes adjust until I could see to walk by the ambient streetlight through windows.

I'd just slipped back to the living room when a shadow popped through the kitchen window and dropped to the floor. I came so near to shooting that shadow that I still get cold chills if I think about it, but for some reason I shouted, "Freeze", and the shadow said, "Alex?"

I grabbed her by the shoulders and shook her until her teeth rattled, hugged the breath out of her, and then gave her a shove. She plopped down to sit on the kitchen floor.

"I guess you're mad at me, huh?" Paloma asked.

"Mad, mostly scared, flabbergasted. Do you realize you came within an eye-blink of being dead?" I sat down on the floor beside her and lowered the hammer on the pistol. My hands were shaking.

"I was trying to be quiet so you wouldn't notice me."

I very nearly lost it. She came within an eye-blink of being busted in the chops that time. Chances are you're not in favor of men hitting women, and usually I'm not either, but it wasn't really me sitting there shaking, and her gender had nothing to do with anything.

"Paloma, I came in here for the purpose of shooting any shadow that moved. I had the hammer back on the pistol, and at that point you don't even have to pull the trigger, you just have to think about it, and baby, I was thinking about it." I noticed that my shoulders were shaking too, and then I felt tears on my cheeks. Not very manly, and I couldn't tell you why. Maybe anger, frustration, relief, hysteria?

Women are right, tears do help sometimes. At least these got me back to reality. "What the heck did you come in here for?"

"I guess you really didn't want to shoot me, huh?"

"Don't count on that. Pull a dumb stunt like that one more time, and I won't mind in the least. Why did you do it?"

"There's a bracelet and a locket in my bedroom, and I want them."

"My God, I'll buy you all the bracelets and lockets in the world. You didn't have to risk your life for them."

"I know you would, Alex." She reached to squeeze my hand, and I had stopped shaking. "Only you can't buy these. These were my mother's, and sometimes in the night I wouldn't mind dying for them. Mother loaned them to me, and I was wearing them the night I came home to find our house had been bombed. They're the only things left of my family."

Chapter 15

"Kablowie," Renaldo said.
"I was thinking more like a Karumph."
"Sounded to me like a snap."

Paloma wasn't very impressed by our inventive genius, she was much more interested in buffing and shaping her nails. The wires and tape that Renaldo and I had spread on the table rated a wrinkling of her patrician nose. Maybe the little puddles of vinegar and the dusting of soda had something to do with her attitude too.

The problem with car bombs is that you need a car, and cars are hard to drag through the jungle and drop down air vents. The substitute car that Renaldo and I cobbled together in our hotel room didn't look like much, but I was proud of it. We used a twelve-volt dry cell battery and a nice new ignition coil from NAPA. That was the easy part.

To make a coil work, you have to simulate alternating

current. Cars do it by interrupting direct current with a set of points, and the pulses act on a coil like alternating current. We only needed one spark, so we only needed to zap the coil one time, but we wanted it to happen a good while after we left the area.

Radio Shack had a nice big relay with contacts that stuck out a couple of inches. A spring held the contacts apart until they were pulled together by the coil, or in our case, pushed together by a balloon. We taped the relay into a coffee can and stuck a balloon in on top of it. We used a little plastic oiler with a spout, taped the spout into the neck of the balloon and filled the oiler two-thirds with vinegar. When Renaldo said "Go", I dumped in a tablespoon full of soda and screwed the lid down tight.

Vinegar is your basic acid and soda is alkali. In the process of combining into a base, they make a lot of bubbles and release a lot of gas. Maybe when you were a kid you made one of those little boats using that principle for propulsion? In the boats, you put a few drops of vinegar into a spoon full of soda. The foam squirts out the back, and you have a jet boat.

We used the foam to blow up a balloon. The balloon squeezed the relay shut, and we got a nice blue arc off our coil. This was our tenth try with a hundred percent success, and we'd tried it upside down and sideways with equal results. Not many modern inventions can claim a record like that. The only reason Paloma was able to belittle our "Kabooms" with her "snap" was that we hadn't connected it to the bomb yet.

The next problem was that we now had two packages, the bomb and the portable car. I figured I could schlep one of them through the jungle by shoving it ahead of me, but both would be a problem, and I liked the idea of keeping the bomb and the power supply separate until the last minute. We considered solutions, and Renaldo hired Juan (*in absentia*). Paloma would have crawled through the jungle, but I didn't want her to, and that was purely sexist.

The next morning Renaldo drove back to La Guiara and picked up a very willing Juan. By noon, the four of us were sailing down the Libertador Vargas. Renaldo and Paloma sat in the front seat of the Chrysler, dressed like affluent tourists. Juan and I sat in the back seat, wearing our new oilskins and sweating, while Renaldo and Paloma in front shivered in the blasting air conditioning. When we got close to the drop off point, Juan and I taped up our wrists and ankles. Renaldo slowed down. Juan and I jumped out, me carrying the bomb, Juan carrying the timer.

Renaldo and Paloma sped away toward a nice dinner somewhere a couple of hours up the road. We didn't want the Chrysler going back and forth in the area until long after the excitement had died down. Juan and I hunkered down in the brush, doused our selves with Off, and crawled into the jungle.

The fact that I had been there before didn't help a heck of a lot. The route looked familiar, but all routes, or roots, looked equally familiar. We progressed inchworm fashion, shoving our bundles ahead a foot and then pulling ourselves up to them. I favored the left arm a little, but not too badly. I'd pay for it later, but it was working okay at the moment.

I came to a four-inch log lying crosswise and very nearly set the bomb on it before I realized it was moving. Juan could see the snake past me, and he was getting excited.

He wasn't afraid of it. I got the impression he wanted to kill it and eat it, maybe right there on the spot, judging by his gestures. If he'd been in front, I think he might have taken a bite out of it. I held the bomb up for a long, long time before the snake tapered off and disappeared.

We missed my original spot and came to the corner of the fence away from the gate. Maybe I was subconsciously angling away from the driveway and guards. When I spotted the fence through the trees, I signaled Juan to stop and left the bomb with him while I wriggled forward for a peek. I didn't do it like a seal wriggling off an ice flow. By my count, there were eighteen automatic rifles waiting to shoot at the first snapping twig, so we weren't snapping any. We were moving one limb at a time and testing the spot before we put weight on it.

Down the back side of the fence, I could see a guard shack at the far corner. It was the size of two phone booths tacked together, with windows on three sides. The guards had a view of the corridors down the two rear sides of the compound, but now I knew the purpose of that outpost was to guard the lane that wound through the jungle from the airport.

We crawled along the brush pile to my original vantage point, took a tack for the vent, but missed it and went too far. We turned around and came back. I was trying to squeeze the bomb past the vent before I realized what it was. Juan wriggled around to the other side of the vent, and we unscrewed the mesh from the top. Juan got excited again at the smell from the vent, and I think he said "cocaine." I couldn't be sure because he mouthed the word silently with considerable exaggeration.

The little roll of duct tape was zipped inside my jacket. I believe that stuff is commonly called "duck" tape and relied on heavily by rednecks. They use it to repair everything from pickup trucks to shotgun stocks. In the aviation world, we call it "hundred-mile-an-hour tape", and many a Piper Cub and Taylor Craft are patched with it. This particular roll was called "Sure Tape," and we had cut it down to ten feet for easy transport.

Juan held the power supply and the bomb together with the coffee can lid on top while I taped them. I touched the two wires from the power supply together and held them for several seconds to be sure no residual spark was stored. They didn't arc, but I hated to take them apart anyhow.

I took a deep breath, screwed the two wires onto the terminals on the bomb, and covered the terminals with tape so they couldn't short against a metal pipe. Juan was getting eager to leave, but he was too noble to leave me alone. I put the last foot of tape over the coffee can lid so there were tabs hanging down on both sides of the plastic cover. Juan held the lid carefully so the tape tabs didn't touch anything.

The vinegar was already in the oilcan. I took the soda out of my shirt pocket, dumped it in, and gave the oiler's lid a couple of screws. Juan handed me the lid to the coffee can and disappeared toward the road. I jammed the lid onto the can, taped it down and dropped our invention down the vent.

I had hoped the bomb would drop fifty feet, but I heard a clunk about ten feet down. I was already scooting after Juan, and not nearly so quietly as we had come. Our priorities had changed since the soda hit the vinegar. We made several hundred feet before the explosion came, and if we'd met a snake, we'd have crawled right over it.

Maybe it wasn't a *Karumph*, but it sure as heck wasn't a snap. The trees above us took a dip from the wind at the same instant we heard the explosion. The next moment, the jungle disappeared in a dust storm. The air was filled with white powder, not unlike Renaldo's office had been after the barrage, but the powder wasn't cocaine. It tasted like concrete, and Juan was more excited than ever. He seemed to be shouting "bauxite," or maybe he was mouthing the word. I couldn't tell; I was deaf.

We felt our way through the dust, slowly and silently again. We were fifty feet from the road when a truck stopped and men jumped down. We froze and quit breathing. A terrible swishing through brush commenced, but it seemed to be along the edge of the jungle. The swishing worked both ways away from the truck, and pretty soon the truck started up and moved a couple of hundred feet farther from the driveway.

Automatic fire blasted into the jungle fifty feet away from us, and I wondered if the snake had foolishly reared his head. A heck of a lot of vehement Spanish was being shouted from the road. Juan put his white-powdered lips next to my white-powdered ear and whispered something, but it was in Spanish, too. He seemed fairly calm though, so whatever he was hearing must have been good news.

The search party whooshed right past our entry point, so apparently we hadn't left any tracks or dropped any calling cards. They beat the bushes for a quarter of a mile before the racket stopped. The truck turned around and roared back past us. We didn't hear any more noise, but I wasn't positive they hadn't left a guard. Juan seemed pretty sure, and started crawling toward the road again, so I followed him. I unsnapped my rain jacket for a quicker grab at the pistol in my belt.

We stayed off the road, hugging the edge of the jungle, and hiked double time through the brush for ten minutes before we stopped to take off the oilskins. Air on our bodies again felt almost as good as a shower. We folded the rain gear and carried it with us because we didn't want anything left that could indicate how we got in. Then too, perish the thought, we might want to use it again some time.

For an hour we hiked along the edge of the road, hiding in the brush when a car passed. I guessed we'd covered five miles before the Chrysler slipped smoothly up behind us. Renaldo lowered his window and stuck his head out.

"Hey, you guys really made a mess back there. There's white powder all over the road for a mile." Renaldo was in much too good a mood.

Juan started spouting machinegun Spanish again while we climbed into the back seat. Paloma turned around to inspect us and wrinkled her nose.

"What the devil is Juan so excited about?" I asked.

Renaldo translated. "He thinks you're a genius. You've discovered the richest bauxite mine in all of Venezuela."

"Did you stop to damage the gold mine in the process?" Paloma wondered.

"Probably not much," I had to admit. "The vent pipe wasn't very deep, but it doesn't matter. Julio will have to retaliate."

"Yep," Paloma agreed. "That's the true meaning of honor among thieves. An eye for an eye, and a tooth for a tooth. All scores must be settled."

My stomach growled, so I thought to ask. "Did you find a decent dinner along the highway?"

"Oh, Alex, it was divine. They catch a fish like a trout in Lake Maracaibo and rush it up to the restaurants every afternoon." That from Paloma.

"The best part," Renaldo put in, "was dancing with Paloma. Alex, if you could see Paloma do the mambo, you'd forget about bombing mines and concentrate on the important stuff."

"Okay," I said, "next time we trade places." I looked at Juan. His clothes were caked with sweat and dirt, and his hands and face looked like a Japanese Kabuki dancer's. I assumed I looked the same, and it occurred to me that I had never seen Renaldo with dirty hands.

"Sure thing," Renaldo agreed. He brushed some imaginary dust off the cuff of his immaculate suit coat.

We came to the junction with the Autopista, and Renaldo started to turn right toward Caracas. Juan let out such a frantic tirade in Spanish that Renaldo slammed on the brakes, spun the wheel, and peeled away toward La Guaira.

"What's the matter?" I asked.

"Juan can't stand to be away from Maria for another minute. If we don't get him home soon, he'll die of grief. Alex," Renaldo half turned in his seat, "will you tone down that stomach rumbling? It isn't very polite, you know."

Chapter 16

Paloma and I sat on the couch nursing Cokes while Renaldo called Julio at his secret emergency phone number. We didn't want Julio getting the idea we had skipped, particularly with the cash. Renaldo listened to Julio for a long time, holding the phone several inches away from his ear. I could hear Julio shouting at the phone from my perch on the couch clear across the room, but he had reverted to Spanish.

Renaldo hung up the phone and slouched over to join Paloma and me. He scooped his Dr. Pepper off the coffee table when he passed.

"You were right about the traitor. Hey-suse' had a boating accident about the same time our offices were being shot up." Renaldo had the weight of the world on his shoulders, so he sat in an uncharacteristic slouch to drown his problems in Dr. Pepper.

"Hey suse?" I asked.

"Yeah, J-e-s-u-s, Hey-suse'. He was out in his boat, and the gas tank exploded. Barnabas is vacationing in Brazil."

"So?" I asked.

Paloma explained. "Brazil is Uncle Dom's territory. That's why all his goons speak Portuguese. There's government pressure against the cartels n Brazil. That's why Uncle Dom is moving here. No innocent Venezuelan would vacation in Brazil. They all go to Las Vegas."

"Okay, so Barnabas is the traitor, and you're down to one partner. Did Julio notice the bomb at the mine?"

"Oh, he noticed all right. He knows Dominic was behind it, but he thinks the bombing was an inside job. He figured out it had to be done by the guards at the back corner of the compound, so he had them shot. He tortured them first, trying to find out where Dominic is hiding, but apparently they didn't know."

"Working for Julio can be hazardous to your health." I was having a tiny twinge of conscience for setting up the guards.

"Oh, they don't mind. They expect to get shot. They're like the guys who kept volunteering to go back to Viet Nam."

Paloma got up to pace and make her provocative feline silhouette against the hotel room windows. "If Julio can't find Uncle Dom, then he isn't going to hit him."

"Maybe we could give Julio some directions, anonymously, of course," Renaldo suggested.

"It would have to be very anonymous. It would be hard to explain if Julio figured out where it came from," I pointed out. "Anyway, Julio is our main problem. Uncle Dom has no interest in you beyond your partnership with Julio."

"Yeah, but how about me?" Paloma asked. "If Uncle Dom knows I'm alive, he'll find me in Tibet, and if he successfully takes over Julio's operation, he'll be the richest man in the world with nothing to do but look for me."

"He may not know you're alive." I offered. "The only one who knew for sure was Paco, and he's not talking."

"Do I dare take that chance?" Paloma had a good point. Renaldo and I might solve Renaldo's problem, but neither of us could leave a lady in distress. Particularly not a lady who was wearing shorter and shorter skirts and tighter and tighter sweaters, and pacing with the grace she must have shown in her mambo dancing.

"Maybe we can flush Uncle Dom out of his fortress. We do have a couple more bombs." I was volunteering again, but this time not for a crawl through the jungle.

We hit Renaldo's house at midnight. That time Paloma stayed in the car. I used the flashlight to check out the sink very carefully and concluded that no one had stepped in it since Paloma and I left with the car bomb and the jewelry. The thing about booby trapping doors is that after you set the trap, you need a way to get out yourself. That's how I knew to check Renaldo's window. The bomber couldn't have left by the front door after he strung the string, but he could just lean in the window to arm the bomb on Renaldo's bed.

I decided that the bomber hadn't been back, and was still waiting patiently for me to climb in through Renaldo's window. When would I ever learn to stretch a thread across portals so I could be sure? I stood in the sink and played the light around the kitchen floor before I jumped down. Nothing but floor tiles that were beginning to show a dull layer of dust. I didn't see any footprints in the dust, and I took that as a good sign.

The bomb still sat behind the front door with the string I had cut attached. I knelt down on the carpet with the flashlight and studied the bomb. The trip mechanism was a lever two inches long with a hole in the end for attaching a string. I could see marks on each side of the lever that looked as if a piece of tape had been peeled off. I searched around the carpet and found the wadded remains of a two-inch length of duct tape. I brilliantly deduced that the proper method of transporting the bomb was to tape down the lever.

Renaldo had a tin box of Band-Aids in his medicine cabinet. I took six of the biggest ones and bandaged that lever down like Torquemada had bandaged my chest. That reminded me that it was about time for a bandage change on the chest. I had thrown away all the miscellaneous ones when I showered after my crawl through the jungle, but I was still wearing the original red badge of courage on my bullet hole, and it wasn't white any more.

I debated, and decided to take along the bomb from Renaldo's bed too, thinking it would probably save me another trip back through the sink. That bomb appeared to be identical, and had the gray sticky leavings from tape beside the lever. I wondered how the bomber had managed to get the duct tape off without the tape pulling the lever. Band-Aids seemed much superior to duct tape because they had the little square of gauze over the lever, and wouldn't pull on it when they were removed.

I stacked up the two bombs and set them on the drain board while I climbed out the window, then reached back in for them. I set the bombs on the back seat of the Chrysler and sat down between them, one hand resting idly on each of the levers just in case the Band-Aids fell off and the levers tried to jump out. We made it back to Caracas in one piece and stashed the bombs in the closet where a maid wasn't apt to inspect.

We ordered breakfast from room service at the El Conde. Renaldo went shopping while Paloma pulled my bandages off, and I took a scalding hot shower. Renaldo came back with hydrogen peroxide, bandages, a ball of twine, and a twelve-ounce fishing weight. Paloma doused my shoulder with hydrogen peroxide, pronounced me infection free, and stuck on new bandages.

I took on the role of lead scientist. "The idea is that when the bomb hits the ground, the fishing weight breaks loose and pulls the lever. The trick is that the bomb has to be upside down when it hits so that the weight will pull the lever out. We're going to make sure of that by attaching a parachute."

Renaldo solemnly handed me his handkerchief.

"Not a monogrammed hanky dummy, unless you have one that says Julio."

Paloma brought a napkin from the room service cart. We tied twine to the four corners of the napkin and tied it underneath the bomb.

"Okay, now the next problem is that the bomb is going to hang upside down and we don't want the weight pulling the lever until it hits, and especially not when the parachute opens."

Renaldo brought out the shoebox that his new oxfords had come in. We tied the weight to the shoebox, and taped the string to the side of the box with four inches of duct tape. Renaldo held the box overhead and dropped it. The weight stayed firmly attached. We tried three inches of tape and dropped it again. One side of the tape pulled loose, but it wasn't convincing.

"Okay, two inches." That time the weight broke loose and hit the floor with a clunk. "Again," I said, "and this time shake it before you drop it."

Renaldo shook, and the weight pulled loose. We used two and a half inches of tape to attach the weight to the lever and then wrapped the parachute around the whole thing so the lever couldn't pull out before the parachute opened.

The kid at the flying service was still reading a Spanish magazine, this time *Playboy,* and didn't look up when he pointed toward an old Cessna 172. Paloma sat in back with the bomb in her lap, and translated us out of the control zone.

It was another picture-perfect day; ocean just visible on our right, snow-covered mountains growing up out of a green carpet on our left. The hills below us undulated gradually higher, covered with a variegated green jungle. We passed the crest and followed it down, staying a thousand feet above the mountains until we saw the glint of Lake Maracaibo ahead of us.

I judged where Uncle Dom's hacienda was by the shape of the lake and chopped the power. We skimmed across the jungle behind Uncle Dom's fortress. A quarter mile from the cliff, I dropped the flaps and slowed us down to sixty. The controls felt mushy, but the plane wasn't going to drop out of the sky.

Coming from behind the cliff, we were still going to be 500 feet above the swimming pool. I would have loved to be higher. We were close to the "low and slow" recipe for disaster, but we didn't know what the wind might do to our parachute, and we didn't want to drop our bomb in the jungle.

I slowed down because the door opens forward and the rush of wind is holding it closed. That's why the car doors that opened front-to-back in the 1930s came to be called suicide doors. They were convenient for ladies to step out of if the car was stopped, but if a door opened when the car was moving, the wind ripped it right off.

It's also why you should keep your head if you notice that your two-year-old has opened the car door while you're driving. If you just keep on truckin', the wind will hold the door shut, and the kid couldn't get out if he tried. If the driver panics and slams on the brakes, the door will swing open and throw the kid clear across the street.

When the jungle carpet ahead of us appeared to be ending, Renaldo released the door latch, and the door opened half an inch. He turned sideways in his seat and got his feet against the door. By pulling against the yoke with his left hand and the seat back with his right hand and shoving against the wind, he managed to get the door open a foot and held it.

We staggered over the last row of jungle right at stalling speed. Uncle Dom's swimming pool flashed at me and I hollered, "Now." Paloma chucked the package out through the door. Renaldo relaxed and pulled the door closed. I didn't want to make enough noise to cause people to look up, so I added just enough power to make us fly again. We circled to watch. Our parachute opened and drifted down. It sailed across the courtyard and bumped onto the hacienda's flat roof. Nothing else happened.

I added more power and started to climb out, thinking we'd go back to Benny's and work on Plan B, when Paloma said, "Wait a minute." A breeze had picked up our parachute and was dragging it across the roof. For a moment the parachute fluttered past the edge of the roof while the bomb sat still, then the package teetered and fell onto the patio.

"Kablowie," Renaldo said.

"Sounded more like Karumph to me."

"Well, it wasn't a snap," Paloma admitted.

The front of Uncle Dom's roof looked as if it had been bitten by a dinosaur with a twenty-foot maw, and I was pretty sure no glass on the property was left unbroken. We went back to discuss Plan B with Benny, anyway.

Chapter 17

Benny delivered. Renaldo proposed a toast to victory. "Do you really think we killed Uncle Dom?" Paloma asked.

"About one chance in ten thousand." I estimated.

"Well, we have one more bomb. Who shall we deliver it to?" Renaldo swizzled the ice in his Hurricane.

"Let's wait a day or two and see what happens." I suggested. "Just where is Julio holed up?"

"Darned if I know," Renaldo frowned. "I handled the books and the money, but it's not like Julio trusted me."

"Does Barnabas know?" I asked.

"Oh sure. Julio and Barnabas grew up together."

"Okay, then Uncle Dom knows. Maybe we can follow him." I took a big sip of rum and felt the erudition flood in. "So far, we've seen five or six of Uncle Dom's cars, and they've all been black sedans. Can we count on that, Paloma?"

Paloma considered for a long sip. "Probably. Uncle Dom himself drives a white Lincoln, but there were always black sedans around."

"I didn't notice any cars at the hacienda." I pointed out.

"They were there. That long building on the other side of the swimming pool is a five-car garage, but that's for Uncle Dom and his personal guards. If he orders a hit, it won't come from there."

"Just where will it come from?" I asked.

"Well, I would guess Barcelona. That's the closest major airport except Maiquetia, and that would be too obvious."

"You mean he's flying these guys in?" I asked.

"Well, if Renaldo's count is right, you've killed at least sixteen of his men so far. It must be time to fly in more from Rio or Sao Paulo."

"Sixteen?" I hadn't thought of myself as that bloodthirsty.

Renaldo rushed to defend his mathematics. "There were nine men in the cars that shot up the office, all dead. Three guys went off the cliff in the car that brought Paco, and of course Paco. Then there was the sniper..."

"Okay, okay, you're just being a little careless with the credit. How many men does Uncle Dom have, anyway?" I asked Paloma.

"Well, approximately whatever the current population of Brazil is. I doubt there's anyone in the country who wouldn't jump at the chance to work for him."

"Then we're not going to win this war by attrition. We've got to go straight to the top."

"Of course. That's why it was such a good idea to bomb Uncle Dom." Paloma set down her empty glass, and Benny was there with a fresh one. Benny had caught our rhythm, and was doing a superlative job of keeping us supplied.

"Does anyone really vote for staking out the airport at Barcelona and following the cavalry to find Julio?" Renaldo asked. Renaldo finished his Hurricane, and Benny was there. Benny had also brought me another rum and Coke, but I was several sips behind schedule. I chugged to catch up and handed Benny the empty.

"We know we can find Julio later because we've got at least a half million of his dollars. Meanwhile, maybe Dom will get lucky. Paloma, does Uncle Dom ever leave the fort?" I asked.

"Well, normally he would if there was an opera in Caracas, but right now, I doubt it."

"So, if we want him, Alex has to crawl through the jungle?" Renaldo asked.

"Hey, buddy, remember it's your turn, but there has to be a better way. Maybe we could pose as window repairmen who just happened to hear the blast."

"Or pizza deliverymen. How the heck does Dominic get his groceries up there?" Renaldo was thinking better and better.

"He'll send someone down for them, but forget that. There would be three men, one to drive and two with automatic rifles." That sounded familiar.

"How would you guys like to go on a picnic?" I asked. "Maybe we could even camp out a little, do some bird-watching, appreciate nature, get away from all our problems."

"Sounds like fun," Paloma agreed, "but why do I get the feeling you have a particular place in mind?"

"Might be you have a suspicious nature. I just thought it would be nice to get away from it all and relax for a few days. Let's find a nice scenic spot, just kick back for a while and do some bird watching."

"At Lake Maracaibo?" Paloma and Renaldo asked in unison.

"Sure, why not? Let's find a sporting goods store and pick up some camping gear."

Renaldo made hold-it-down gestures to Benny, so he let us finish our drinks without bringing more. Renaldo stopped by the bar to sign the tab, while Paloma and I wandered out to the bell desk and ordered the car.

Renaldo knew the sporting goods store because he'd bought his Beretta and the rain slickers there. Naturally, when we walked in he greeted the clerk with his hearty, "Hi Gus. How's that kid of yours?"

Gus looked up with a smile, happy to see his old buddy Renaldo. Gus was wearing Coke-bottle glasses, and had the first bald head I'd seen in Venezuela. He rushed to shake Renaldo's hand, showing almost as many teeth as Juan had. Gus brought Renaldo up to date on his family problems while I pulled Paloma over to look at the counter displaying pistols.

"Ever shoot a pistol?" I asked her.

"Are you kidding? I'm a drug-runner's daughter. I used to carry a .32 automatic in my purse."

"How about that .38 Patrolman there? Can you handle that?"

"Want to see my Annie Oakley impressions?"

Gus and Renaldo caught up on the family news and wandered over to join us. I bought two S&W .38 revolvers and a box of copper-clads. We also bought a six-pack of Deep Woods Off, and another rubber rainsuit, small size, for Paloma.

"Don't we need sleeping bags and stuff?" Renaldo asked.

"No thanks. Remember this is a bird-watching excursion. I have every intention of doing my sleeping in a king-sized bed after a hot shower."

"Party pooper," Paloma pouted.

"Hey, you guys go right ahead. You can sleep on a bed of nails, if you like. I'm only telling you what I have in mind. Next stop, hardware store, then maybe we should buy you adventurers some hardtack and pemmican."

At the hardware store we picked up rope, a tarp, a hacksaw, a couple of Swede saws, a bolt cutter, all the usual bird-watching paraphernalia. Maybe in this age of political correctness, the Swede saws are called "bow saws" or some such innocuous descriptive term, but whatever you call them, they are great for cutting brush and small trees.

We took turns driving along the coastal route, and during the evening I was wishing we had rented a convertible. The mountains on the left, occasional panorama of the Caribbean on the right, and the sweet-smelling jungle whiffing by almost had me believing we were on a holiday jaunt. Funny about the jungle. When you're in it, it smells like I imagine a mushroom farm does, but taken as a whole, from a little distance, it smells like a tropical fruit farm.

After the sunset exploded and the views went away, Paloma crawled in the back seat and took a nap. After my next turn at the wheel, I traded her places. When the sun came up again, we were driving slowly through the jungle past Uncle Dom's driveway. The driveway was a dirt-and-gravel lane blocked by a massive steel gate that opened from the middle, and was posted with "Keep Out", "Private Property","Prohibido", and "No Trespassing" signs. An eight-foot chain-link fence stretched away in both directions. The signs seemed redundant.

Paloma stopped the car, and I jumped out to inspect the lock. Thirty-foot trees almost met over the road and the lane. They were dripping here and there with a tropical version of dew, and had a musty, unoccupied smell like a house that has been vacant for a hundred years. Birds were waking up and screeching at each other, but I couldn't see any of them.

The lock on the gate was a padlock the size of a grapefruit. An oval window cut half into each side of the gate, had steel bars the size of my wrist with a chain running around them, and the padlock closed the chain. It hung in front of the oval so it could be reached from either side of the gate. The chain put me in mind of D-8 Caterpillar tractors and logging operations on the Washington peninsula. Attacking that chain or the padlock with bolt cutters and hacksaws would be a full-time job for a month.

Renaldo got out to stretch his legs. We strolled up the highway away from the coast, figuring that any emissaries from Uncle Dom would turn toward the coast and the causeway to Maracaibo. Paloma idled the Chrysler along behind us while we searched for a spot to hide the car. It was obviously going to have to be on the downhill side, because Uncle Dom's fence was going right along with us on the uphill side.

A quarter-mile from the driveway, we found a massive old monkey pod tree that had shaded a tennis court-sized patch, so the brush wasn't too thick. The borrow pit that ran beside the road was only a foot deep and a couple of feet wide. I could see a stand of bamboo sticking up out of the brush behind the tree like an inverted green waterfall. Like Brigham Young when he saw the Great Salt Lake, I announced that this was the anointed spot.

Renaldo and I unpacked the bow saws. Paloma drove away to hide the car for a few hours, and no doubt practice her mambo. Renaldo slipped on a pair of soft leather gloves, lest a blister detract from his manicure. We hacked a driveway at an angle to the road so that if you looked straight at it there was nothing to see. Mostly we just cut the small trees and left them standing because there wasn't room for them to fall down.

We worked our way around behind the umbrella tree, and cut a dozen eight-foot lengths of good-sized bamboo stalks. We think of bamboo as light, but that only applies to dried and seasoned fishing poles. When it's green, bamboo has a lot in common with lead pipes, but we dragged our logs through our driveway and stacked them under the brush next to the borrow pit.

Paloma came back a little after noon to find us sitting on the ground, exhausted and filthy, with sweat making streaks through the dirt on our faces. We climbed into the Chrysler and guzzled cold Cokes from the cooler while Paloma raced for the causeway and that bed I'd promised myself in Maracaibo.

We'd only worked half a day, and that the cool half, but I've loaded mail into airplanes all day long in the arctic and been in better shape. Renaldo was so tired that his mustache drooped below his chin. He closed his eyes and started to snore as soon as the Coke cleared the dust out of his throat. The tropical custom of taking a siesta at midday is based on very sound principles of survival.

We stopped on the causeway for ten minutes while an oil tanker the size of a small city went past the drawbridge. I decided that if anyone was in hot pursuit, the causeway was not the way to escape.

Maracaibo isn't a big tourist town, but we found a hotel that looked inviting and was willing to have us, even though our efforts to scrape off the dirt with paper towels hadn't been very effective. Renaldo did his trick again with a banded bundle of hundred-dollar bills, and we procured three rooms with baths.

After a one-hour bath and a two-hour siesta, we met in the lobby downstairs. The lobby was aging gracefully, like a Victorian dowager. It had class, but from the previous century. We wandered through nearly-deserted streets, automatically drawn downhill toward the lake, and the Avenue Milagro. We were attracted like moths to a row of flaming torches next to a thatched and woven open-air restaurant on the lakeshore.

Paloma had been right about the fish. They were reminiscent of the best of trout, and these were served ten feet from their natural habitat. The house wine was a Chardonnay from Chile, the perfect complement to the fish and the sunset. Renaldo and Paloma chatted up the staff in Spanish, and I kept my gringo mouth shut. The dinner check was exactly half of the listed price, or would have been if Renaldo hadn't tipped outrageously.

We wandered along the waterfront, arm in arm, more like a rose between two thorns than like the Three Musketeers. We met a few other tourists, passed some convenience stores, and finally came to an open *farmacia*. Paloma bought a book called *The Outlander* by Gabaldon. I found a Donald Westlake and a Dick Francis. Renaldo picked up a small handful of Louis L'Amour. We bought a long, tapered candle and a can of lighter fluid, and called it a night.

Chapter 18

We woke up a bunch of birds, and what I think should be called a "flight of monkeys," while we shepherded the car into our freshly-slashed driveway. We filled the borrow pit with our bamboo logs, drove the car across, dug most of the logs out, and hid them again.

Renaldo and I walked ahead, picking up small trees and brush and standing them up again behind the car. Our driveway arced around behind the umbrella tree and stopped at the edge of the bamboo thicket. We covered the car with the tarp and stood the bushes back up around it. From the road, the jungle looked normal.

We strolled across the highway carrying the picnic basket, books, and the six-pack of Deep Woods Off. Except for the guns in our belts, we looked like any bird-watching expedition. We built ourselves a people-sized blind behind a rotten log right beside Uncle Dom's driveway, got comfortable (within reason), and lost ourselves in Scotland, New York, and the Old West.

The morning warmed up and wore out. Sun worked its way across the road. The jungle had stopped dripping and was steaming. We were in shade, but the trees just seemed to hold in the steam, and not a breath of air was moving. We passed the Off repellent around like teenagers sharing a bottle. Westlake's Dortmunder was about to walk into a reservoir wearing scuba gear when the expected black sedan drifted quietly to a stop just inside the gate. The passenger in the front seat jumped out, carrying his rifle and looking around for trouble. He was dressed in black with pegged pants tucked into engineer's boots and a shirt that looked western.

We quit breathing while he selected a big key from a ring and opened the padlock. He swung the gate, and the car eased through. He replaced the padlock giving it a tug to be sure. He climbed back into the car with the rifle barrel sticking out the window in our direction while the car sped away toward Maracaibo.

"Well, was that the grocery run?" I asked Paloma.

"Groceries, booze, or maybe just after the morning paper, but definitely a trip to town."

I took our new taper candle over to the gate, lit it, and carefully let the wax drip into the padlock until the lock was nearly full. That lock held over three inches of candle so I guessed it was gummed up pretty well.

Lunch was egg salad sandwiches and Cokes that we had picked up from an all night restaurant that looked to me like a Denny's, but was named Popo's. We set our artillery in our laps, and Paloma showed Renaldo the niceties of the pistol. Like any good general, I outlined the battle plan.

"When I say *now*, we each shoot one of them. I'm on the left, so I'll take the left-hand one of them. Renaldo, you shoot the middle one, and Paloma takes the one on the right."

"What if I miss?" Renaldo asked.

"Then we'll all get raked with one of those Uzis, so don't. Just hold the front sight in the notch of the back sight and point it at his middle."

Renaldo made several dry runs, pointing the gun at this and that and pronouncing "pow!" when he had it lined up. Paloma and I went back to our books. Westlake's Dortmunder commenced to get into trouble as only Dortmunder can. We were starting on our third can of Off when the sedan came back.

The guy riding shotgun, so to speak, jumped out, gun in hand, and tried to jam the key into the lock but it only went in halfway. He tried some other keys, went back to the right one again and pushed harder. A minute ticked by, one torturous second at a time. The second rifleman climbed out of the back, carrying his Uzi, and walked over to grab the keys. He pointedly selected the right one and shoved, then shoved again.

The first sounds were grumbles, quickly escalating to shouts. Each clearly blamed the other for the problem, and the original key man patted himself down, apparently looking for another key ring. The driver climbed out, brandishing a key ring of his own, and marched over to settle the argument.

When the driver stuck his key in the lock, the three were lined up perfectly. I raised the .357 and said, "Now."

Renaldo jumped up, waving his gun and shouted "Freeze." Paloma and I each kicked the back of one of his knees, and Renaldo fell backward behind our log just as the line of automatic fire stitched through the brush behind us. The next pass of stinking hot whining bullets blew most of the top off of our log.

I dove past the end of our log, and while I was still rolling, shot the one with his rifle raised. The other rifle came up pointed at me, and Paloma shot that guy three times in less than a second. The driver had jerked an automatic out of his belt, but he was more interested in running back to the car than in shooting us. Paloma shot him neat and clean on the run with what I assumed was her Annie Oakley impersonation.

We both turned on Renaldo. He was flat on his back, pistol extended overhead, staring up in shock at the line of bullet holes across a tree behind him.

"Shall I shoot him now?" Paloma asked.

"Go ahead, unless this is 'be kind to dumb animals week.' Just what in blue blazes did you think you were doing?" I asked Renaldo.

"I couldn't just shoot them in the back with no warning. It didn't seem right. It wasn't sporting."

"Shooting people isn't a sport, you dumb schmuck. Do you think we're in one of those Louis L'Amour books? We had one-tenth of one second to stay pretty safe, and that's why we were going to all shoot at the same time. Why we're all still alive now, I really don't know."

I restrained the urge to give Renaldo a good kick while he was down. The line of bullet holes behind him seemed to be sending him enough of a message. I ran to the lock, poured it full of lighter fluid and set it on fire. It blazed up for a moment, and smoked a little when the wax caught on fire. I held it by the bale and dumped out a nice stream of melted wax, then poured it full of fluid again and relighted it.

The lock was too hot to touch. I used my handkerchief for a hot pad and shook out the final drops of wax. Paloma brought the driver's key ring. I ran back to the lunch box for a can of cold Coke and doused the lock. It popped and sizzled, but cooled off. I poured the last of the lighter fluid into it for some lubricant and tried the key. The lock popped open.

The gate swung easily. I tossed the keys to Paloma and held the gate while she drove the car through. Renaldo was still sitting on the ground behind the remnants of our log, shaking his head. I grabbed him by the arm and jerked him up. He seemed to wake up and ran for the car. He climbed in back, and I noticed that Paloma had tossed the two automatic rifles into the back seat. I dragged the bodies off the driveway, in the interest of neatness.

I closed the gate and draped the chain, but put the lock on only one end of the chain and didn't snap it closed. To a casual observer it would appear locked, but if it were pushed, by a car in a hurry to leave, for instance, it would swing open. I jumped in beside Paloma and reloaded our pistols, while she drove up the driveway toward the lion's den.

The Uzi that had ripped apart our log was leaning against the back seat. I reached over the seat to pick it up. It had two clips taped together, opposite ends up, so reloading was a matter of just removing the clips, reversing them, and snapping them in again. I held the Uzi up next to the window the way its former owner had held it.

We came out of the trees onto a flagstone courtyard. The hacienda, sans porch, was on the left, swimming pool straight ahead, and a two-story building on the right had a line of six garage doors. Bare sticks bordered the house next to the swimming pool. The leaves and roses were floating in the pool, along with a couple of boards from the porch.

Apparently we cut a laser beam in the last fifty feet because an alarm buzzer went off, but it was immediately silenced by someone. We were the right car at the right time with the right number of people, and apparently we passed an inspection by persons unknown and unseen.

Paloma pulled up next to the wreckage of Uncle Dom's porch and stopped. I looked around the back seat, but saw only Renaldo, sitting with his shoulders hunched, idly playing with his unfired pistol.

"Shouldn't there be some groceries somewhere?" I asked.

"Maybe in the trunk?" Paloma suggested.

"I'll check," I volunteered. "I look more like a hired gun than you do."

Paloma handed me the car keys. On second glance, she did look like a hired mercenary, one who has been through a nasty campaign in a swamp. There's something about a jungle, even just sitting in the edge of it. "One touch of nature makes the whole world kin." All who step into the jungle are going to come out dirty.

Paloma was wearing a sort of jumpsuit, solid black. It accentuated her golden bronze complexion, not to mention her feminine figure, and made her eyes snap, almost as black as her pulled-back hair. Now she was charcoal gray. Her eyes were still snapping, but not because of the color.

I took the keys and jumped out, carrying the Uzi and trying to look relaxed but dangerous. I never doubted that someone was watching, but couldn't spot who or from where. We were parked ten feet from the wreckage of the porch. The swimming pool beside us looked inviting, but not just at that moment. Across the pool, a line of white changing shacks had their doors closed. Behind us, the six overhead doors were closed on the garage. The second floor appeared to be apartments, or maybe a dormitory. A line of windows along the second floor looked like mirrors in the sunlight, so Uncle Dom had replaced the glass.

Two Gucci shoulder bags were propped in the trunk and one had a stalk of celery sticking out the top. I brilliantly deduced they were the groceries. I grabbed the bags, one in each hand so the Uzi was pointed downward in an un-business-like attitude.

I slammed the trunk shut with my elbow. Paloma got out, so I handed the Uzi to her. Renaldo was still sitting, looking like a five-year-old with coal in his Christmas stocking. It finally occurred to me that Renaldo had never really been shot at before. True, the two of us dodged a few bullets that time in New Orleans, but those were coming one at a time from a .38 and missing us by ten feet. The fusillade that destroyed their offices had been stitching the ceiling and Renaldo was in the outer office for most of that attack. When someone is up close and personal, doing their best to blow you away, the effect can be profound.

As to actually shooting someone himself, that thought had probably never even occurred to him before today. He was happy to encourage me to do it, but that's an entirely different thing. He just had an understandable case of buck fever. I intended to rag him about it, but I really didn't want to attack his manhood.

"You stay here and guard the car," I told him. "Our lives may depend on it." That seemed to help a little. He put down the pistol and picked up the other Uzi. Paloma and I walked around the plastic-covered veranda, up a couple of improvised steps, and into the house without being challenged.

I didn't know where the kitchen was, so I set the groceries in the hall and got the .357 in my hand. The hall was wide enough to drive a car through and was carpeted like the Royal Palace, but it was dark. Maybe our bomb had cut some electricity. "The Toreador Song" from *Carmen* was blasting from a block down the hallway, and Paloma charged toward the sound. I was three steps behind her, having trouble keeping up.

Paloma banged the music room door open with her shoulder and jumped inside. I caught up and bumped into her. I was looking everywhere for Uncle Dom, but the only occupant of the room was a skinny kid who looked around twenty years old. He stared at Paloma for a second with something like shocked horror, or horrified shock, got control of himself and gave her a big smile. He touched the remote control in his hand and the music stopped in mid swagger.

"Paloma, my darling, you're alive. How wonderful."

I was still looking around for Uncle Dom, but Paloma was focused on the kid. The kid got up and reached out a friendly hand to her, his right.

"I thought you were lost in that terrible accident that killed your parents." The kid had Paloma's eyes, and a good roof of black hair, slicked back like Julio wore his, but mostly this kid had a smile. I could envision bronze statues melting at his feet from that smile. I wasn't buying it, but I doubted that any woman could resist.

"You had nothing to do with that terrible accident?" Paloma asked.

"Of course not, darling. Your father was my elder brother. I looked up to him like a family god." The kid, who I was starting to figure out was Uncle Dom, took one more step toward Paloma, apparently really wanting to shake her hand. His left hand had been behind him, and it swung out naturally when he stepped, but I saw the glint of a gun in it and jerked the .357 up.

I was way too late. When an Uzi does its thing in a closed room, it pounds your ears, and then your eyes, until your head threatens to burst, but Paloma wasn't letting up. She held the trigger down until that monstrosity ran out of bullets, and even then she was trying to shoot some more.

Usually, when an automatic rifle is fired, particularly in Rambo-type movies, the shooter sprays it back and forth, like a gardener watering with a hose. Not Paloma. She was focused on the kid, and I think every one of those bullets went straight into his chest. There was no need to check his condition. I grabbed Paloma's elbow and dragged her back toward the door.

"Come on," I shouted. "It's time to go." Both of us were temporarily deaf, but she got the idea, dropped the empty rifle, and we ran back up the hall. Suddenly the entire front of the house exploded. The front door banged open and swung crazily with a row of bullet holes across it. We dove and buried our noses in the carpet. Bullets were flying past us, chipping plaster off of walls and ceiling and screaming away down the hall.

I rolled over on top of Paloma and held her down flat. It was more instinct than design, but if I was going to die, that wasn't a bad place to do it. The shooting stopped abruptly. Certainly another Uzi was empty, and I wanted to get to the front door before the gun could be reloaded. If that one had the clip taped double, it would take about three seconds, so I dived for the door.

I hit the carpet again at the doorway with the .357 leading the way, hammer back. I almost collided with what was definitely a corpse. I crawled right over him, still looking for the shooter. There sat Renaldo in the car, gun barrel sticking out the window, and laughing, maybe hysterically. Three more corpses were piled up outside the door, and the front of the house had been sprayed with the garden hose technique. The only spots on the wall without bullet holes were the spots where the guards had been when Renaldo cut loose.

That took longer to tell than it did to see. I was already halfway to the car, and Paloma was passing me, headed for the passenger side. I had just started the car when a fat little guy with a fringe of hair around a shiny pate came out of a dressing room beside the swimming pool. He fit my image of Uncle Dom a lot better than the kid in the music room. He was stark naked except for a .45 automatic in his hand, and the automatic was swinging our way.

"Shoot him, shoot him, shoot him!" Renaldo shouted. I didn't need his advice. The guy took two more steps with bullet holes in his forehead and fell into the pool, floating face down. Fortunately for me, Renaldo's Uzi was empty because he had it sticking through my window, three inches from my ear and was jerking on the trigger.

"Who the hell was that?" Paloma asked.

"That was partner Barnabas." Renaldo removed the Uzi from my face.

I popped the clutch and screeched around in a circle toward the drive. When we blasted past the garage, two of the overhead doors were opening. I had the throttle on the floor, so I kept it there.

I hadn't noticed how crooked the drive was on the way up, because I'd been busy loading the revolvers. It was a lot straighter after we went down, because I ripped out a chunk of jungle on almost every curve. I slammed the gate with the bumper, skidded through, and locked up the brakes. We threw gravel all the way out to the highway before the car stopped.

"Run for the car," I shouted. I grabbed the gate on the back swing, jerked it shut and clicked the padlock home. I didn't have any wax handy, so I fired a shot into the general area of the tumblers. It didn't hurt the lock much, but it should have bent something. I could hear an engine screaming down the drive toward us. Paloma and Renaldo were disappearing up the road toward our stashed rental. I jumped back into the sedan, backed it around to block the gate, and jammed it into low gear. I took the keys, hit the door lock button and ran for the road, just as two cars careened around the last bend from the driveway.

It was instinct again, not heroism, but when I got to the highway, I ran the other way, toward Maracaibo, because the guys in the cars could see me. I heard a terrible avalanche of gravel and then two crunches. I think the first car hit the gate, and the second banged into the first, but that's a guess. I ran fifty feet down the road and dived into the jungle on the down hill side.

I did my seal act again, pretty darn fast because I wasn't being quiet. I was getting as far as possible from the highway. WWIII erupted from the gate. I guess they were trying to shoot the lock off, but that solid steel grapefruit wasn't going to give in easily. I judged I'd gone a hundred feet, and the jungle was already muffling the sounds of gunfire. I turned parallel to the road and wriggled back toward the rental.

Our umbrella tree stuck up above the brush, and I zeroed in on it. A commotion was still coming from the direction of the driveway, so I took a chance that noise was not a problem. I called to Renaldo that it was me crashing through the brush, and please not to shoot. Renaldo and Paloma were sitting calmly on the hood of the car, sharing a Coke. Our last one, it turned out. When I stood up, Renaldo extended it to me. I was grateful for the inch of warm liquid that was left.

Renaldo seemed to have grown about a foot, and had a lot more chest on him than usual. Even his mustache seemed to be proud of itself.

"Four of them," he announced. "They ran right past the car, headed for the house, and when they lined up, I let 'em have it."

"Good job. Undoubtedly saved our lives." I decided not to mention that he had very nearly shot us a hundred times in the hallway. Okay, okay, those were .9mm slugs, so each clip only held thirty, but on the receiving end it seemed like hundreds. Maybe the guys who make the Rambo movies got their Uzi impressions from the front. They spit more bullets out of an Uzi than Gene Autry used to get out of a six-gun.

The shooting from the driveway stopped, and was replaced by a series of metal-rending crashes. I think they were trying to move the car out of their way by ramming it. A final crash, louder than the others, was followed by an engine screaming and then a horrible, ear-splitting screech. Two cars careened out of the driveway, and raced away toward the Maracaibo causeway.

"Maybe we should go home over the mountains," Paloma suggested.

"Good idea," I agreed, "nothing like exploring new territory."

Paloma backed the car out while Renaldo and I walked ahead of her, tossing brush over as we went. We dragged our bamboo bridge into the borrow pit, and Paloma backed onto the highway.

Renaldo climbed in front beside Paloma, so I settled down in back. Renaldo half turned in his seat with a worried frown.

"There seem to be quite a few bad guys left. Maybe we should stick around and shoot the rest of them?" Renaldo had not only recovered from his buck fever, he had developed a blood lust.

"No need," I assured him. "No matter how big or how long a snake may be, it dies when you cut off the head, and Paloma most certainly did that."

Chapter 19

Renaldo called Julio from our adjoining suites in the El Conde in Caracas. Julio had calmed down a little, but still seemed to be boiling angry. From my seat on the couch, clear across the room, I could hear the spout of vitriolic Spanish that was blistering Renaldo's ear. Renaldo put down the phone, strode into his bedroom, and came back with a pocket-sized notebook. He read something to Julio, listened to another tirade, and hung up the phone. He looked a little wilted, probably from the heat of Julio's shouting.

Paloma was sitting on the couch with me, wearing black again. This time it was a short straight skirt and a short-sleeved blouse. I didn't think she was in mourning for Uncle Dom. I thought she wore it because it showed off, in breathtaking contrast, her flawless bronze skin.

Paloma scooted closer to me, and patted the spot the other side of her for Renaldo. He sat next to her and adjusted the crease in his slacks. It struck me that the two of them were a nicely matched pair, they made me look the slob that I am.

Renaldo translated the phone conversation to English for my benefit. "Julio wants to make a shipment, war or no. He's in his fortress, up in the mountains somewhere, and Uncle Dom's goons raided him yesterday. Julio stood them off, and any survivors from Dom's army hightailed for the border, but he thinks Dom is getting too close. The gold is piling up at the mine, and Julio wants to get it out of there before Dom hits the mine again."

"What did you tell him?" I asked.

"I told him *Montezuma's Pride* would be off the coast of Aruba on its way to Miami the day after tomorrow."

"Doesn't Julio know that Uncle Dom is dead?" Paloma asked.

"Apparently not. Maybe Uncle Dom's henchmen don't know either. At least they're going ahead with whatever had already been planned."

"So Julio will be moving the goods from the mine tomorrow?" I asked.

"Probably tomorrow night. He likes the highways and La Guaira to be pretty quiet when he moves."

"How would you guys like to take a little swim?" I asked.

"To Aruba?" Renaldo looked doubtful.

"No, only part way. Can we get some snorkels from your buddy, Gus?"

"Sure, snorkels, scuba gear, whatever you want."

"Bathing suits?" I asked. "Especially for Paloma. She needs the sexiest suit we can talk her into."

"Why Alex, you dirty old man. I didn't think you had noticed I was female."

"Oh, so that's it. I knew there was something different about you, I just couldn't put my finger on it."

"And you'd better not try. If you want me in a sexy outfit, there's a little number at that store where I worked in La Guaira that I wouldn't be caught dead in."

"Then that's the one we want. I certainly don't want you getting caught dead. Maybe you can pick up some trunks for Renaldo and me, too? If yours is all that good, maybe you'd better make ours boxer style."

We picked up a couple of masks with snorkels, but skipped the fins as too obvious. We stopped by the hardware store again for fifty feet of three-eighths-inch aircraft cable, a handful of cable bugs, and two half-inch wrenches. That wire rope is wonderfully flexible, and extremely strong for its size. Probably there was a time before hydraulics when large aircraft used cable to connect controls. Several light airplanes use a small flexible wire rope for controls, but I don't think I've ever seen any as large as our three-eights inch.

We hit La Guaira at ten o'clock the next morning and moved back into the penthouse at the Venezuelan. Apparently reservations were not necessary. Paloma took a handful of bills and went shopping. She was back in an hour with straw hats, a couple of big beach bags, towels, and boxer trunks for Renaldo and me. She had a little package for herself, but she wasn't about to show us, and she slammed her door when she went into her room to change.

Renaldo and I used a couple of cable bugs to make a running loop in one end of the aircraft cable and got the roll stuffed into one of the beach bags, along with the snorkel masks.

Our bathing trunks had pockets that held the rest of the cable bugs, and we tied the wrenches to the drawstrings. We ordered a picnic lunch from room service, and packed that in the other beach bag with the towels.

Paloma came out of her room wearing a wrap-around skirt and a peasant blouse with an elastic band around the top. She was in white for a change, but her outfit was printed with larger-than-life hibiscus in various neon colors. Renaldo and I pulled pants on over our trunks. We all put on straw hats and set out to play tourist. We strolled down the avenue along the waterfront, watched the fishermen, and gloried in the bright sunshine, but kept our hats on because we walked right under Julio's office window and the glass had been replaced.

We were enchanted by the tiny strip of sand between the oil-covered rocks next to pier three on the side away from the PT boat. We climbed down, spread our towels, and relaxed in the sun. Renaldo and I slipped off our pants and shirts to sit in our bathing trunks. Paloma unwrapped her skirt but kept it on and pulled her blouse down off her shoulders like a tank top.

I was struck for the ten-thousandth time by what a truly beautiful woman Paloma was, and for my money she really didn't need to reveal any more. I was totally mesmerized already. Her lines were smooth and harmonious, like a Brahms lullaby, but with the immediacy and vitality of Vivaldi.

I was also struck by how sickly white my skin was compared to Renaldo and Paloma. I'm no houseplant, and my face and forearms get a good bit of weather. They even look tanned, more from windburn than sun, but that's by Alaskan standards. Next to Renaldo and Paloma, my skin had an ugly bluish cast to it.

The locals gathered around on the sidewalk, pretending not to look at us. After a while they decided Paloma wasn't going to take off any more, so they wandered back to their fishing. I waded out a few feet and ducked down to get wet. The water wasn't hot by any means, but I've had showers that were colder. Once I was wet all over it wasn't bad, and when I stood up, the sun felt marvelous.

Renaldo waded out and we engaged in a little horseplay, splashing water on each other and then on Paloma. She screamed nicely, and a couple of the locals wandered back to watch again. I tossed a handful of water on Paloma, and she retaliated by throwing the beach bag at me. She missed me and it landed under the dock with a splash. I dumped out the cable and the snorkels and tossed the wet bag back at her.

She screamed at me again, jerked on a bright red bathing cap, ripped off her clothes and dived into the water. She was just a flash, a couple of bright red strips of cloth barely clinging to a perfect body. She stayed underwater until she was thirty feet out, and came up swimming hard to get away from us.

She swam halfway out to the PT boat, rolled over to float on her back and take a rest. Renaldo and I slipped under the dock, and no one noticed. I thought a couple of the old-timers were going to follow Paloma down the dock, "Prohibido" sign or not.

Renaldo and I slipped on the snorkels. I looped the cable around my neck and over my right shoulder. We dogpaddled along under the dock and passed Paloma on our way to the boat. It was hard to rip my eyes off that floating perfection and keep on going. Paloma saw us pass and started a lazy backstroke paralleling us, but thirty feet out from the dock.

When we got close, I was surprised at how big that PT boat really was. From the street, it looked like a launch. From under the dock beside it, it looked like an ocean liner. Renaldo stopped to tread water next to a very large, very solid-looking piling. I handed him the coil of cable, took the running loop, and dived down under the stern. The props were protected by tunnels, and were a heck of a lot bigger than I had imagined. The only protrusion I could see on that smooth hull was the rudder, but I was out of air.

I hugged the hull and came up underneath it, blew the snorkel clear and gulped down air. Renaldo, hidden under the dock, was motioning frantically for me to dive again. I could see where the expression "frogman" came from. His eyes, at least the way they looked through his mask, were twice normal size. He wanted me down in a hurry, so down I went, one breath too soon.

I tried hanging the loop over the rudder and pulling it down under the thing but the loop wasn't big enough. When I tried to pull more cable Renaldo pulled back. The loop slipped off the top of the rudder and I had to dive fast to catch it. I grabbed the loop just as it passed the bottom of the rudder.

From down there, I could see that a lot more rudder was sticking down below the hinges than there was above them. I passed the loop under the rudder and pulled it up. That worked. I got the rudder lassoed (maybe in Venezuela it's lariated), and got back under the dock with just enough air left to blow the snorkel.

All that Glisters // 189

We wrapped the end of the cable around Renaldo's piling, four feet under the water, and clamped it solid with the cable bugs. Renaldo held the cable tight and put the little bails under it. I put on the flat part of the clamps and the nuts, and cinched them down with the wrench. It wasn't that easy.

We each had three of the little cable clamps in our swimsuit pockets. Renaldo dug out the first one and dropped it. Underwater it fell in slow motion, but when I tried to grab it, the water pushed it away from me, and down it went. He dug out another one and hung onto it by the bail. I unscrewed the nuts, removed the grip plate, and promptly dropped one of the nuts. We put it on anyway with only one nut. I dug a clamp out of my pocket, took off one nut and put it on the first clamp to finish that one. I took off the other nut and the grip plate and tried to hand the bale to Renaldo, but he fumbled it and the bale disappeared.

We came up for air. I dug another bug out of my pocket, took off the nuts and plate and handed the bale to Renaldo. Nothing to it above water. We dived back down and put that one on, but when I tightened the second nut, the wrench slipped off the nut and out of my hand. I dived after the wrench and followed it down until the water got too murky to see. I was surprised that there was forty or fifty feet of water under the dock.

We went up for more air. Renaldo dug out his last cable bug, unscrewed the nuts and ceremoniously handed me the nuts and the plate. He untied our spare wrench from his drawstring and slapped it into my hand, like a relay racer passing a baton. We got that one on in good shape, and I stayed down to put the last cinch on the first two clamps.

Actually two cable bugs are enough to hold any cable.

The third was just for insurance and good measure, and maybe to prove we could do it. When I came up, Renaldo looked the question. I dug the last clamp out of my pocket and released the clamp and the wrench to Davy Jones' locker.

I sneaked a look at Paloma, still floating on her back, and it was well worth the swim. Renaldo and I paddled our way under the dock back to the rocks and dumped the snorkels. We climbed onto our little beach and dried ourselves off without the slightest glance from anyone.

We unpacked sandwiches and those ridiculous little plastic wine glasses. Renaldo opened the bottle of wine, whistled at Paloma and waved the bottle for her to see. She rolled over and did a lazy crawl back to join us. A funny thing happened when she got close. I suddenly got embarrassed. I picked up the largest towel, spread it wide, and waded out to meet her.

She exploded out of the water like a Northern Pike after a lure, and leapt straight into the towel. When I had the nerve to look, she was demurely wrapped, and we waded the last few feet together. Renaldo held out a glass of wine to each of us. We lounged for a while, ate the prosciutto sandwiches and drank the wine, Paloma staying well wrapped. The fishermen went back to fishing.

"Why did you motion me to dive too soon?" I asked. "You darn near drowned me."

"A sailor was leaning on the rail right above you, and I was afraid he was going to fall in."

"A sailor." Paloma was either angry or mortified. "There were half a dozen of them, and the way they leaned out, it's a wonder the boat didn't capsize."

"Well, I did tell you you're too beautiful for ordinary men to endure." I reminded her.

"Huh!" She gave me a haughty sneer, but she softened a little. "Thanks for the towel, Alex. That was really sweet."

"Hey, I did that for my benefit. Otherwise I'd have had a heart attack."

We finished our lunch and gathered the debris back into the bags. We were pretty well dried off. Renaldo and I pulled our pants on, and Paloma pulled that female trick of dressing inside her towel. We climbed back up to the sidewalk and continued our stroll.

Renaldo was thinking again, usually, but maybe not always, a bad sign.

"What happens next?" he wondered.

"Well, exactly what and when is up to Julio, but in very broad terms, I'd say that Mineral Corporacion is going to lose one of its last two partners."

"We still have a bomb left," Paloma suggested. "Maybe we can deliver it to Julio."

"Maybe," I agreed, "but Uncle Dom's goons tried and couldn't, and they knew where he's holed up. We don't."

"Actually, what I was thinking," Renaldo continued, "was how excited Juan got over that bauxite when you guys bombed the mine. If the last partner left standing happens to be me, then the gold mine will close and that property belongs to the company. Why not give it to Juan and Maria?"

"I thought Juan couldn't own property." I reminded him.

"Juan can't, but Maria can."

"Do you really have a legal right to do that?" Paloma asked.

"I don't see why not. I signed all the papers for the company when we bought it, so I should be able to dispose of it, assuming that Julio loses interest in the property."

"Well, if you do that, you'll certainly have Maria praying for your survival." Paloma seemed to like the idea a lot. "Maria will probably burn down the local shrine lighting candles on your behalf."

"Well, that settles it. I'll walk up there tomorrow and set up the deal."

"Better date the deed a month from now." I advised. "Even if you do happen to be the surviving partner, it may take a while for all the miners to pull out."

"You and Juan could crawl in and bomb the mine again," Renaldo suggested.

"Damn it, I told you it's your turn next."

"Oh, well, we'll think of a better way."

We strolled into the hotel and punched the elevator button. We got some curious glances from the desk clerk, but Renaldo waved at her and she waved back.

In the suite, we showered and got cleaned up. I noticed that my skin wasn't quite so white as it had been, but the new color was pink, not tan. The rest of me pretty well matched the new scar on my shoulder. It was healing nicely and was no more tender than my pink legs and belly. I wandered out to the dining table and settled down to find out how Dortmunder was going to dig up a buried treasure forty feet under water. Renaldo came out and joined me, but he had abandoned Louis L'Amour and purloined my Dick Francis.

Paloma had washed her hair and came out wearing a towel as a turban. The back of her neck was so feminine and sexy that I almost forgot Dortmunder's problems. Her bone structure was light and elegant, but strong, like the frame of a glider. She settled down on the couch with *The Outlander* and immediately went back to Scotland. I had to reread the same page twice to get Dortmunder's entourage sorted out again.

At seven o'clock, we called room service for dinner. Paloma ordered scallops, and Renaldo ordered fried oysters, but I wanted another Crab Louie. Paloma went back to her room and came out with her shoulder-length ebony hair brushed to its high sheen again. That was sexy too, but I could handle that and concentrate on those big juicy chunks of crab.

The wine lasted better than usual, so we each had a full glass left when we settled down to read after supper. The only interruption in our quiet evening was when I had to chuckle out loud at Dortmunder. I finished the book and the last sip of wine together. The wine was warm, but nothing can spoil the last sip of a good Vouvray. Nothing can spoil the ending of a Westlake book, either. Renaldo was still working on my Dick Francis, but had laid out a Louis L'Amour for me. I'm probably the only person alive who has never read Louis, and I decided to keep that distinction. I wandered over to the window to survey the waterfront. The avenue was lighted, but subdued and deserted. The entrance to pier three was dark, but the PT boat was showing some lights from the cabin, and the running light on the mast was lit.

The bay had a little more swell to it; long low rollers sliding in instead of the usual disorganized chop. The moon must have been right above me because I couldn't see it, but it was lighting the waves into alternating furrows of light and shadow. They reminded me of the plowed fields on a Japanese truck farm in Western Washington where I worked summers during high school vacations. That was in the Puyallup River valley where the black topsoil goes down forever. We plowed the residue of each crop we harvested four feet deep with a twelve foot ganged plow behind a D-8 Cat. Those deep furrows, wet and black at the bottom and drying lighter on top, had the same rhythm as the bay; except the furrows were standing still, and I was moving along on the Cat.

I leaned my forehead against the cool glass and thought about the boy I was then and the man I had become, and it seemed to me that nothing much had changed. Any changes there might have been were probably not improvements. Trading Western Washington for Alaska had seemed like a great adventure at the time, but that was over. Alaska was just home now.

Silhouettes of palm trees against the moonlit ocean were exotic and tropical. I reflected that ice would be running in the Kuskokwim now, unless there had been a cold snap and the river was already frozen over. The palms and the grass along the avenue had a warm comfortable look to them. I could see that it would be pleasant to stroll down there, no parka or mukluks required.

It occurred to me how similar jockeying a helicopter is to jockeying a D-8. Both hands and both feet are busy, and full body coordination is required. I just might have decided that I was out of my mind to call Alaska home, flying every day so I could afford the fuel oil to keep my little cabin warm. I might have decided that, but I noticed a string of cars zipping down the avenue.

"Here they come." I said.

Renaldo and Paloma dropped books and ran to join me at the big picture window. The first cars drove past the pier to stop, and the next ones fanned out, so the effect was like a herd of musk oxen circling horn to horn around their calves. In this case, the calf looked like an armored car. It stopped at the pier and backed down it all the way to the PT boat. There wasn't much light or movement anywhere; nothing to attract attention. I began to see men leaning across the cars with rifles, then more men walking along the pier, watching the water.

The transfer was by hand. Several men were off-loading white bags from the van and handing them over the railing onto the boat. The bags were disappearing below the deck, fast and efficient like a well-tuned assembly line. I lost count early on but there were several hundred bags, and they looked like twenty-five pound flour sacks to me.

Bags stopped coming. The van doors closed, and the van eased back down the dock. Sparks from diesels, like red fireflies, swarmed out of the exhaust stacks on the boat. Lines were cast off and water behind the boat churned white. The stern dipped down, or maybe the bow rose, and the boat pulled away from the dock.

The next second it really was the stern that dipped down, and it nearly went under water. We heard the bang and the screech of tearing metal from a block away, right through our plate glass window. The boat made a crazy swing away, then rammed the dock and stopped. We could see men running and lines being tossed.

The hatch burst open on the rear deck and the white sacks started coming up fast. They were piling up on the deck until more men got there and started tossing them across to the dock. The van stopped and reversed. It blocked our view, but it seemed to me that the boat was getting lower and the sacks were being tossed up higher and higher to get them on the dock.

The sacks stopped coming up, and men scrambled out of the hold. The van doors closed, the van rolled back off the dock, and the entourage reformed itself and sped away down the avenue. Men were still running around the boat, attaching more and more lines to the dock. The stern that had been even with the dock was now right at water level and the rollers were washing over it.

Activity on the dock slowed down. The boat was leaning out away from the dock but it seemed to be secured and wasn't sinking any more. Suddenly men were leaping off the boat and running down the dock toward shore. The dock very slowly, almost majestically, leaned over toward the boat. Our cable must have broken the piling as well as jerking the rudder out by its roots. In any case, the boat was holding up the dock and the waves were washing over both.

The bow of the boat stood straight up in the air, towering over the waves, and then slowly went down. It made a shrinking black triangle in the moonlight, then the waves rolled uninterrupted across the missing section of dock and the vacant slip.

"Wow," Renaldo breathed, "Julio is really going to be mad at Uncle Dom now."

Chapter 20

Renaldo set off early to visit Juan and Maria on his philanthropic mission. Paloma was curled up on the couch, still in Scotland. I decided that one way or another, we didn't need the rental car anymore, so I went down to the desk and returned it. Julio was still embattled against Uncle Dom, but I figured that we needn't be. It ought to be safe to use the Jaguar again, assuming it was still in the parking garage under the offices.

I strolled out into the sunshine, and walked on the grass beside the sidewalk under the palm trees. I was confirming my impression that, gold mines aside, Venezuela was a nice place to be. I turned down the avenue past pier three. The gap where the dock was missing had an ugly, raw-wound look to it with splintered edges. Forty feet of planking was missing, and one piling, the mate to the one that Renaldo and I had banded, was sticking up naked. The fishermen were just setting up shop for the day. A couple of them ventured down the dock past the "Prohibido" sign.

Renaldo's office building looked to be back to normal, and a guard was loitering around the entrance. I rounded the corner and walked past the entrance to the parking garage. I didn't see any bullet holes, and the usual guard was on duty in his little kiosk. I decided to conclude that Dom's attack hadn't included the garage, and the Jaguar was probably safe.

I wandered back up to the suite, and Paloma and I had the soup-and-sandwich special sent up from room service for lunch. The soup was clam chowder, New England style with big tender chunks of clams, and the sandwich was a BLT that made a nice combination. I would have admired the wonderfully ripe Venezuelan tomatoes, only now I knew they came from California, and that took out the magic.

Paloma didn't notice lunch. She stayed nose-in-book throughout and even got a tiny smear of mayonnaise in the corner of her mouth. I wondered about licking it off for her, but decided she wouldn't notice that either.

Renaldo came floating in on Cloud Nine, virtue oozing from every pore. I wondered if he realized there was a very real chance he wouldn't live out the week. If he didn't survive the week, I wouldn't either of course, but somehow that didn't seem quite so important. Funny how Renaldo had that effect on people.

"Success?" I asked him.

"Certainly. Pretty hard to miss on that one. Maria now owns fifty hectares, complete with mineral rights. The house, too, what the heck. I'm getting to like hotel living."

"You did mention the slight possibility of bombs, arson, murder, and mayhem?"

"I think Juan had the picture. He'll probably inspect the house board by board before he lets Maria and the kids into it."

"Okay, one problem solved, and Paloma might be out of the woods. Now we just have your worthless hide to worry about."

"You think I should call Julio?"

"I think he might be expecting it, but remember, you're calling from Caracas and you don't know anything about the boat sinking."

"What boat?" Renaldo picked up the phone and made the call. For a change, Julio must have used a normal tone of voice, because I was hearing only Renaldo's side of the conversation. Not that it mattered; it was still in Spanish. Renaldo and Julio talked for quite a while. When Renaldo hung up, he looked thoughtful.

"Julio wants me to arrange an airplane charter to haul the gold out. Seems something went wrong with his maritime plans."

"Really? He didn't say what?" I wandered over to the window and looked down at the gap in the pier. The random chop was back in the harbor and sunlight winked from waves where the PT boat had been.

"No, just that he's changed his plans. He also wants me to come back to work tomorrow. Business as usual, he said."

"Did he mention Uncle Dom?"

"No, subject never came up. He did mention that I should bring the cash back and get it into the safe again. He wants me to call him back when the charter is arranged."

"What time does he want you to come to work?"

"He didn't say, but I suppose around nine. Does it matter?"

"Not much. Can you set up the charter for him?"

"Oh sure, no problem. Couple of phone calls."

"Okay, set up the charter for late afternoon, maybe just before dark?"

"Can do. Anything else?"

"I think maybe we should buy Maria a gross of votive candles."

Renaldo went back to the telephone and I went shopping, but didn't buy candles. I found a clerk at the marine supply who spoke English and bought a thousand-foot spool of ten-pound-test filament leader. I had to convince the clerk that I was running a charter fishing operation, and couldn't be bothered with the 250-foot spools he wanted to sell me.

He went back into the storeroom, and eventually emerged with a thousand feet of line in a cardboard box that acted as a spool. It had a plastic ferrule on top with the line fed through it, so in theory all you had to do was pull and the whole thousand feet would feed out nice and smooth. I also picked up a new roll of duct tape.

When I got back to the suite, Renaldo and Paloma were sharing a bottle of champagne with a third glass on the table for me.

"What's the special occasion?" I asked.

"This is the last night with Julio's bankroll and no accounting. I thought we should try to spend a little."

"Just might be the last night for a heck of a lot more than that." Somehow I was irritated with Renaldo for not being scared, even though I would have advised him not to worry if he had asked.

"What say we go out on the town?" Renaldo suggested. "You still haven't seen Paloma do the mambo."

All that Glisters // 201

That's when I noticed that Paloma was wearing a new champagne-colored cocktail dress in some fabric that gleamed and clung provocatively. I guessed it might be silk. Certainly "smooth as silk" came to mind.

I realized I had misjudged Renaldo. He knew very well that this might be his last night on earth, and he wanted to use it in the best possible way. Watching Paloma do the mambo suddenly seemed like a very good way to spend this night. We finished the champagne, danced our way down in the elevator, and grabbed a taxi to a club Renaldo knew in Maiquetia.

Champagne flowed and the lobster tails were done perfectly, which means the chef didn't do anything to them except broil them just enough and serve them up with a quart of melted garlic butter. A Caesar salad was a major production at our table, and some kind of a dessert came to the table flaming. It wasn't Baked Alaska and it wasn't Cherries Jubilee, but maybe it was the best of both with a tropical fruit salad mixed in.

The real dessert was dancing with Paloma, and as Renaldo had promised, that took my mind off of bombing mines and dodging Uzi's. I led Paloma out for a cha cha and Paloma followed me as if we'd been rehearsing that dance together for years. I'm not really much of a dancer, but I can cha cha.

Renaldo and I spent a month on Guam the time Renaldo planned to open a Japanese restaurant there. The restaurant idea was a bust because the Japanese tourists who flock to Guam eat only in Japanese-owned restaurants. They pay for their tours, meals and all in advance, and their money never leaves Japan. We stayed at the Guam Hilton, and the main thing we did get out of that trip was endless cha cha music rocking the hotel from six in the evening until three in the morning, seven nights a week. If the Chamorros have a national dance, it's the cha cha, and I thought I was pretty good, but Paloma anticipated every move. That dress of hers ballooned wonderfully when she spun, and swished above her knees when she reversed.

When the music ended, I spun her off to Renaldo, and they did a tango you could have named a movie after. Renaldo brought her back to the table. She grabbed a sip of champagne. The orchestra struck up a Latinized waltz, and Paloma dragged me onto the floor. Dancing in space must be like waltzing with Paloma. She was weightless, as fluid and ethereal as the music. I wasn't exactly Fred Astaire, but with Paloma it was impossible to make a mistake.

I dipped her down until her hair touched the floor. She hadn't any bones, she was as flexible as a dream. Renaldo scooped her out of my arms, and I staggered back to the table. The mambo shook the exposed beams, rocked the table, made the chandeliers swing to the beat. A few other couples were on the floor to start, but they stopped and sat down to watch Renaldo and Paloma.

I finally understood the purpose and function of the female body, and why it's built the way it is. In the beginning, God created Eve just so that Renaldo could show off her great-great-granddaughter in the mambo a few generations later. I was surprised smoke and flames didn't ignite under their feet. Paloma's skirt wasn't much below her waist the whole time, and the wisp she wore under it was matching. We laughed a lot, drank a lot, and grabbed the taxi back to the hotel a little after midnight.

When we walked into our living room, Paloma kicked off her shoes and spun in a pirouette that ended solidly against me. She gave me the kiss of my life with a champagne flavored tongue in it, and her breasts burned holes in my shirt. She spun around again, plastered herself against Renaldo, kissed him until he pretended to faint, and did a cha cha into her room.

"Need a nightcap?" Renaldo asked.

"No thanks, I just had one. Better leave a wake-up call for seven." Renaldo and I bowed to each other formally and danced to our rooms. I was waltzing, but I think Renaldo was doing the mambo again.

Chapter 21

I slept better than I expected, and I'm not about to admit what I dreamed, but I was up at 6:30 and had coffee and rolls delivered before Renaldo's wake-up call. Paloma somnambulated her way from her room to the coffee and carried a cup back. She was wearing that same nightie that had fired my imagination the night she gave me the Advil. That was the first time I'd seen her hair disheveled, and it had a nice domestic kind of intimacy to it. I guess that's what's meant by "letting your hair down".

Renaldo came out wearing slacks and a white shirt, his tie loose around his neck. He joined my coffee klatch at the table.

"We checking out this morning?" he asked.

"Well, out of the hotel anyway. I wouldn't want us getting in a rut."

Renaldo nodded and concentrated on buttering a

croissant. Paloma came back for a refill. This time her hair was brushed to a high sheen, and she was wearing her black jumpsuit. It was fresh from the cleaners and did that magic thing to her eyes. I was glad to note she was wearing a new pair of black tennis shoes with good high tops, laced up.

We packed all our new clothes into one suitcase, and put the three rubber rain suits into one of our new beach bags. Renaldo had picked up a black leather valise for the money. He packed the bag full of bills and snapped it shut. Paloma tossed her new bathing suit into a wastebasket. That was wasteful, she could have used it for shoestrings.

I carried our last bomb reverently out of the closet and used a good hunk of our new duct tape to plaster the lever down. I carefully slid the bomb down to the bottom of the other beach bag and set the new roll of filament line on top of it. Renaldo knotted his tie and slipped on his jacket. I stuck the .357 in the back of my belt and covered it with my blue blazer.

We checked around like any tourists leaving a hotel, and carried our luggage down to the bell desk. Renaldo handed the bellman a couple of bills to watch our stuff, and we wandered out into the sunshine, Renaldo carrying the black valise. Paloma crossed the street and headed up the hill to collect Juan. Renaldo and I turned toward the office building. The sunshine was the same as yesterday, but it didn't feel so warm and comfortable.

We turned to enter the building through the parking garage. Renaldo stuck his card in the slot just as though we'd been driving. The guard slid out of his highchair, big .45 automatic in hand, to inspect Renaldo's briefcase. I pulled the .357 out of my belt, but kept it pointed at the floor. No one was threatening anyone. The guard was doing his job by inspecting the valise, and he wasn't surprised that Renaldo's bodyguard should be carrying a weapon.

Renaldo opened the valise, the guard took a look at the green stuff and waved us through with his gun hand. He recognized Renaldo, and apparently Renaldo's arriving with a suitcase full of bills was normal. We walked across the concrete toward the elevators and stopped at the Jaguar. The car was locked, and on the Jag, that meant the hood hadn't been opened.

The door key opens all four doors at once. Renaldo unlocked the car from the driver's side. I leaned in from my side to open the jockey box and found the Beretta was still there. I jacked a shell into the chamber and stuck the little automatic into my pants pocket. We closed the car and walked over to the elevators. The same guard posing as a drunk was still sleeping in his convertible by the elevators, still with his mandolin under a jacket on the seat beside him. We punched the Up button and the door slid open, so we swayed and creaked our way up to Five. The hallway was deserted. I had expected the janitor to be lurking behind the door with his gun hand in his pocket, but he wasn't there. Maybe Julio didn't want too many witnesses to this meeting. Renaldo walked through the door carrying his valise. When I stepped into the office, I beeped again. And again, that same granite pillar grabbed me from behind with a big .45 at my throat.

He jerked the .357 out of my belt and held me. Julio wandered out of his office, all smiles, and reached to take my gun from the guard. He gave the guard a gesture and I was released. Julio swung the cylinder and checked the load, but didn't empty the gun. He snapped the cylinder back into place, and held the gun idly by the grip.

I lounged against the reception desk, shoulders slumped, hands in my pockets. I was just a disarmed bodyguard, temporarily off duty. Julio and Renaldo were giving each other their welcoming smiles, fellow survivors of a dangerous ordeal. Julio reached with his left hand for the bag, and Renaldo handed it over. Julio popped the catch, but he didn't put the gun down. Bundles of bills pouched out of the bag. Julio set the valise on the desk, not particularly interested in it. I hiked my leg up and half sat on the desk.

"I'll go stick this in the safe." Renaldo reached for the bag.

"No hurry." Julio leaned against the desk on the far end from me. We were in the same positions as our day with the surgical team but one desk nearer the door.

"Is it really safe to be here?" Renaldo asked. "No more fusillades coming through the windows?"

"No, I think we're quite safe here. My people found Dominic's place over on the lake. Would you believe that both Dominic and Barnabas were dead? Both apparently shot by persons unknown?"

"Well, thank heaven." Renaldo breathed a big sigh of relief.

"Would you believe there was a sedan smashed up outside Dominic's gate with an empty Uzi on the floor in back?"

"No kidding? Must have been quite a shootout." Renaldo was perfectly calm. I was proud of that boy.

"Would you believe that your fingerprints were all over that Uzi?" Julio asked.

I mentally kicked myself. It hadn't occurred to me that Julio would go in for forensics, or even that he'd find Dominic so soon. Julio was still playing with my .357, not quite pointing it at us, but not pointing it away, either.

I had a good view of the bullets in the cylinder, and they were ugly. Those .357 loads almost reach the front of the cylinder, and the ends are flat. The flat ends emphasized the brute force of that gun. Most bullets are rounded, or even tapered to cut the air resistance and penetrate targets. The slugs I was looking at had so much powder behind them that they didn't need any niceties.

"Renaldo, my lad, you were a fine accountant and a wonderfully gullible patsy, so I don't want you to take this personally." Julio was still smiling, but I saw that cobra lurking behind his eyes again. "I'm grateful to you for taking out Dominic and Barnabus, but then my men found a couple of snorkel masks under six feet of water by the pier. We traced them to Caracas, and they were sold to an hombre with a six inch mustache. Can you guess who that was? I don't resent your attempt to take over. After all, we're just a couple of businessmen, right? We're like that Godfather in the American movie: 'nothing personal, strictly business'."

When Julio thumbed back the hammer on my .357, I hiked my knee up onto the desk and shot him with the Beretta, still in my pocket. I felt a streak of fire run down my leg and the hot casing was burning a hole in my hand, but Julio had a tiny hole right over his heart, and he dropped my pistol. I dived for it and spun to face the guard at the door. He was standing there with his mouth open, and the .45 automatic in his hand was pointed at the desk where I'd been sitting.

I could see what his problem was. He was supposed to shoot me when Julio shot Renaldo, and the poor slob was still waiting for his cue. I put him out of his misery. Renaldo grabbed the money case, and we zipped across the hall to the elevator. When the elevator door closed, I suddenly got claustrophobic. If any alarm was out, we were just too vulnerable. I was slapped by a mental picture of the guard on the ground floor and the drunk in the basement with his banjo.

Renaldo had hit the button for the parking basement.

"Punch 2," I decided. We were already passing three, so the elevator stopped almost immediately. We jumped out, and I led the way, or rather the pistol did, racing down the hall to the stairway. We took the stairs down three at a time, Renaldo's bag of money swinging wide on the corners.

We stopped at the basement door, and I silently shoved it open a crack. The drunk, whose banjo had turned into an Uzi, was uncertainly surveying the empty elevator and wondering if he should shoot it anyway. I dropped to the floor and crawled through the door, Renaldo right behind me. That put several parked cars between us and the wavering guard.

I started to crawl under the first car, but then I flashed on Renaldo's tan suit and all that oil on the floor, and I just couldn't do that to him. I slithered around behind the first car and duck-walked toward the elevator. I could see all the way to the kiosk in front, and the guard who should have been there wasn't. What was there, was a hundred-watt red light blinking, so an alarm had been sent.

The next car ahead of us was a big boxy Volvo that looked solid enough to withstand a howitzer attack. I scooted in between that and a Toyota. Renaldo duck-walked right in behind me, his suit still immaculate. I flopped down on the floor to look under the cars.

I could see the banjo player's feet. He had turned around, his back to the elevator, and the elevator door slid closed. I heard a hushed, frightened exchange of Spanish, and then spotted a pair of toes that belonged to the kiosk guard. He had come over to back up the elevator action, and there seemed to be a disagreement about what to do next.

The now wide awake drunk turned back to the elevator and must have punched the button again. The door slid open. Apparently the elevator was still empty because he went in and the door closed behind him. Kiosk's toes advanced a couple of steps closer to the elevator. I remembered the .45 automatic he had held so casually when we came in, only he wouldn't be so casual now.

I stood up and peeked over the Volvo. No head in sight. The guard must have been crouching down too, and I wondered how long it would be before he looked under the cars. I could have shot him in the foot, but that wouldn't solve anything. Renaldo's Jag was two spaces beyond the elevator so we'd still have to pass him.

I took Renaldo's Beretta out of my pocket. I pretty nearly ripped the pocket off in the process because the synthetic fabric was melted to the gun. I tossed the Beretta as far as I could toward the front of the garage. It bounced off the floor and hit the kiosk with a good whack, but I knew it was a mistake as soon as I let go of it.

My trajectory was right past a row of hanging lights, and the shadow that flicked across the elevator was amplified to ten times normal size. It seemed to travel in slow motion, pointing backward to exactly where it came from. I dropped to the floor and looked underneath the Volvo again. The guard, almost hidden behind that big .45, was also looking under cars, right at me. We shot at the same time, but the projectile that hit me in the face was a concrete chip. The guard simply disappeared.

I motioned Renaldo to stay put. Renaldo was staring at me in shock. I felt the new wasp sting on my cheekbone, and a good bit of blood was oozing out of it, but this was no time to get finicky. I dashed past two more cars and hit the concrete again to get the low view from my new perspective. I could see the guard's feet, and the seat of his pants sticking out behind the front tire next to the elevator.

I considered the possibility of putting a bullet through those ripe haunches that were sticking down, and felt the pain vicariously rip through my own backside. I was still considering it when the elevator door opened and the guard leapt inside. By the time the elevator door closed, Renaldo was passing me and I was right behind him. We piled into Renaldo's Jag, and left rubber all the way to the street.

Paloma and Juan were pacing the sidewalk outside the hotel like a couple of pickets on a line. Paloma had our suitcase in her hand, maybe to hold her down. Renaldo slid to a stop in the loading zone bouncing the front tire off the curb. We jumped out and ran for the luggage. Renaldo tossed another bill at the bellman. We scooped up the bags.

By the time we ran back to the car, Paloma had slid in back, all the way over, leaving the passenger side open for me. Juan was sitting in front on the passenger side, wearing a grin that showed every one of his beautiful ivories. He thought this was great fun. I jumped in back, trying to be a little careful with the bomb in the bag. Renaldo tossed the other bag in my lap and ran for the driver's seat.

The bag that slammed into my lap was way too solid for the rain gear, and I realized we had mixed the bags, but the bomb didn't go off. We were already screeching around the corner to head back toward the highway. The bomb bounced out of my lap and hit the door. Paloma was nearly thrown into my lap. I shoved her off, gently of course, and stuck the bomb on the floor between my feet.

"Hey, Al Unser, are you trying to get us killed?"

"Sorry." Renaldo didn't sound sorry. "There's only one road out of town, and I want to be the first one on it."

Apparently we were, and I didn't see any ominous sedans behind us. The head was off another snake, and the priorities back at the office building would be changing. However, it might take a while for the word to spread down through the ranks, and you never know what some loyal lieutenant might do.

Renaldo whipped us up through the hairpin turns, again with that video game precision, but Paloma wasn't being thrown into my lap anymore. She was looking at me quizzically, though.

"Did you get yourself shot again?"

I remembered my cheek, and it felt sticky.

"Give me your handkerchief." Paloma took charge.

I fished the hanky out of my back pocket, thankful that it was clean. Paloma wet a corner of the hanky with her tongue and held my chin while she swabbed away the blood. It may not have been as sanitary as Torquemada's ministrations, but I liked it a heck of a lot better. She stopped short of actually cleaning the cut. It had stopped bleeding, and apparently I was presentable.

We topped the ridge, and Renaldo let the Jag out. It was still amazing to look over his shoulder and watch the speedometer sitting on 180, kilometers or no.

"What time is the charter set for?" I asked Renaldo.

"Five o'clock, give or take. We're not dealing with a scheduled airline here."

"What time is it now?" I asked.

"Son las once' y triente," Juan answered promptly.

"Five and a half hours before the flight." Paloma translated in case I didn't get the Spanish.

"Great, but we should check in a couple of hours early. We don't exactly have reservations." Renaldo took a broad curve, way too fast, and I could feel the back end getting light. "Preferably alive," I added. "If there's a choice, I'd rather be a little late than piled up beside the road with this bomb in my lap." The mention of the bomb slowed Renaldo down, and we lumped along at a hundred and ten to the junction with Libertador Vargas.

Renaldo pulled off on the shoulder and traded places with Juan. Juan carefully checked his mirrors and pulled sedately out onto the highway. Paloma got the suitcase stashed between her feet, and together we dug the rain suits out of the bag. She checked the size labels and passed one jacket and one pair of pants to Renaldo, then found the small ones and wriggled around to slip the pants over her jumpsuit. With her hair bound tight in a black scarf she looked like a teenager.

I waited until she was through wriggling and then managed to get into my raingear. Renaldo was having a serious debate with himself. He finally slipped off his jacket and removed his tie. He carefully spread the jacket over his seat back and stuck the gold tie tack in the tie. He put the little pin through the original hole in the tie and rolled the tie into the jacket pocket.

When Renaldo figured we were ten miles from the mine, we struggled into the rubber tops and taped up our ankles and wrists with the duct tape. Paloma didn't see why the tape was necessary, so I elaborated on the size and ferocity of the spiders and ants we were apt to meet. I invented a red spider with green eyes and bloody white fangs. Judging by my description, that spider must have weighed half a pound.

Paloma grabbed the roll of tape and went to work taping her pants to her tennis shoes. I stuck the .357 in the back of my belt before I put the rubber jacket on. I decided I'd rather not have it poking my belly later, even if it would take me an extra few seconds to reach it.

Juan pulled off on the shoulder half a mile before our previous entrance point. This time our destination was the airfield, and the farther we were from that gun-sprouting driveway, the better. Renaldo climbed out, carrying his money case. I climbed out carrying the bomb and held the door for Paloma. She slid out carrying the suitcase.

"Huh-uh, leave it," I told her. I handed her the box of filament line. "You're carrying this, and you'll be darned lucky to get this little box through the jungle. Midas hasn't a chance with his money bag."

I tried to take the suitcase out of Paloma's hand, and she cocked it, ready to brain me with it the same way she had with her little overnight case when Maria introduced us on the trail. I was eager to get going before some gun-happy minion of Julio's came by, so I was ready to argue with her.

"Mother's jewelry is in it," she explained. I knew better

All that Glisters // 215

than to argue with that. She dumped the case on the back seat, rummaged through the clothes, and pulled out a tiny leather bag. She ripped her coat open, loosened the drawstring at her waist and jammed the little purse into a pocket on her jump suit. She ran her fingers lovingly over the fabric of her champagne dancing dress and slammed the door.

Instead of pulling away, Juan jumped out and ran around the car. He grabbed Renaldo by the shoulders and gave him a kiss, pretty much the way Maria kissed him. Juan darted back to the driver's seat and sped away. Renaldo had a dazed look. He tried to wipe his mouth with his sleeve, but the rubber wasn't a satisfactory wiper.

I grabbed Paloma by the arm and pulled her into the brush beside the road.

Chapter 22

The Jaguar disappeared in the distance. Two seconds later, a pickup truck came out of the driveway half a mile down the road and turned toward us. We flattened ourselves on the ground, and I desperately scrabbled for the gun, but the pickup sped on by, back toward Caracas or La Guaira. The brush along the road had been cut sometime within living memory, and we hunkered through it. The edge of the jungle that had never been cut, and probably never would be, was a straight solid line, like a stand of wheat next to a swath by a mower.

I had kept the bag on the bomb and the roll of tape on top of it, but had wrapped the bag tightly into a square bundle. It looked like less chance of catching the lever on something that way. I pulled a couple of vines aside, shouldered a slender tree out of the way, and ducked down to crawl under the next one. I did my inchworm trick, shoving the bomb ahead and pulling myself after it.

Paloma was right behind me, shoving her box of line right against my feet every time I moved ahead. Renaldo was dropping back, wrestling his case every which way to get it through the openings. I didn't mind waiting for him. The case must have still contained over four-hundred-thousand dollars, and it had occurred to me that someone was going to have to pay my American Express bill sometime.

We didn't meet any snakes, and after a while I found a trail made by some kind of small animals and it was going our direction. The trail formed an opening through the jungle a foot high and six inches wide, but it helped. The trade-off was quite a few little pellets that looked like rabbit leavings, but they were reasonably hard. I couldn't tell if they smelled or not. The whole jungle had that musty stink that comes with too much birth, living, and death.

When we finally came to the brush pile that bordered the airport, I motioned for Paloma to wait. I left the bomb with her while I slithered through to check our position. My animal trail had led us astray. We hit the runway alright, but barely. We were a couple of hundred yards from the end of the runway, farthest from the mine. There wasn't an airplane on the strip anywhere. I watched a while and didn't see any movement or any guards, but I didn't want to bet they weren't there.

I inched out of the brush pile backward until Paloma said, "Hey, watch it." I squirmed around and found my feet against the bomb. Renaldo had caught up with us. It had to be Renaldo, but I wouldn't have recognized him. Besides the unaccustomed dirt streaked on his face, his mustache was gray from spider webs and dust. He looked pretty happy though, and the moneybag was still intact.

"Leave the money here," I told him.

"Are you out of your mind?" He hugged the case against his chest.

"Don't worry, you're coming back past here."

"What if I can't find it again?"

He had a point there. I remembered my machinations trying to find the vent a second time. I unwrapped the bomb and took out the roll of duct tape. I wrapped the tape around a tree trunk right at the edge of the brush pile and pried the case out of Renaldo's hands so I could wrap the tape once around it. I took the roll with me and crawled twenty feet away from the brush pile, unwinding the tape as I went, taped another tree and crawled back.

"Okay, you guys are going to crawl right past here on your way to the end of the runway. You're going to follow the brush pile. Do you think you can crawl past that tape without finding it?" I rewrapped the bomb.

Renaldo wasn't happy, but he left the case, and we turned to parallel the runway back toward the mine. I was shoving the bomb along, and I had expected Renaldo to take the box of line from Paloma, but she still had the box. She was scooting right along, and Renaldo was still having trouble keeping up. Maybe he was finding it hard to crawl away from the money.

The runway was three quarters of a mile long, and I wanted to be pretty close to the mine end of it. That's a heck of a long way to crawl through the jungle, but 4,000 feet isn't very far at all when you're taking off with a loaded airplane. We crawled for a long time before I left the bomb again and slithered out to take a look. We'd come half way, so we crawled a long time again.

We came to a little clearing. By little, I mean three feet square, but it was enough room to turn around and breathe in. I stopped and set the bomb down. Paloma was right behind me and chunked her box down next to the bomb. She was dirty, and had sweat streaks down her face, but her color was high, and somehow I thought she had never looked more kissable.

Renaldo crawled up beside Paloma and plopped down with his face in the dirt.

"Are we having fun yet?" he asked.

"Not yet. This is where the fun starts. Are there cobwebs in your brain, or are they all in your mustache?"

"Go ahead, I'm listening." He plopped his face back in the dirt again.

I unwrapped the bomb and taped it to a tree. Not neatly, I just wrapped until the bomb was covered, all except the trigger. The original Band-Aids were still over the trigger, and I left them there so the only thing really showing was the loop on the end of the trigger where the string was meant to tie.

"Okay, here's the drill." Renaldo raised his head, so I continued. "Leave the tape over the trigger. When the time comes, I'll jerk it off. You just run the end of the line through the loop, keep it loose, tie it about twenty times and skedaddle. Any problem with that?"

"Skedaddle? Is that like 'run hell bent for leather'?" Paloma asked.

"Pretty much, except do it quietly. You'll be going back the same way we just came, and not carrying anything so you should go pretty fast."

"All the way back to the money?" Renaldo wondered.

"Yep, pick up the money when you pass, but the next time I see you, I want you to be right on the far end of the runway. Unless there are bad guys with guns around, crawl through the brush and get as close to the runway as you can without showing yourselves."

"Okay, we can handle that." Paloma nodded. "Then what?"

"The airplane will taxi back to that end of the runway and turn around for takeoff. If the plane stops, bust out and get in it fast. If it doesn't stop, walk back to Caracas and embark on a life of petty crime."

"You'll be in the airplane?" Renaldo was just making sure.

"That's the plan at the moment, unless I get a better idea."

"Why do I get the feeling all of that is the easy part?" Paloma asked.

"Because it is. The hard part is stringing this line. Naturally, I'll do that."

"My hero!" Paloma made a face at me.

"Well, you guys get to help. We're going to play a signals game."

"Like telegraph, where we all hold hands and squeeze?" Paloma asked.

"Kind of like that. I'm going to take the end of this line and crawl away into the sunset. You're going to hold the box and Renaldo is going to let the line run through his hand. If the line gets tangled in the box, or you need to stop for a minute, give me a long steady pull on the line and I'll stop. I'll wait until I feel another long steady pull, and then I'll start again. Got that?"

"Yep. One pull stop, one pull start again." Renaldo was ready to pull.

"Right. Now it gets tricky. When you come to the end of the line, or if it gets so tangled that you can never get it straightened out, give me two pulls."

"Okay, two pulls means end of line."

"Yep, but don't do anything yet. I'll give you two pulls back, so you know I got the signal. You give me two more pulls so I know you got the signal. Is that too complicated yet?"

"No, I think we can handle that." Paloma wasn't quite sure whether I was putting them on or thought they were idiots, but I did want to get it right the first time, because there wasn't going to be a second chance.

"Okay. After you give me the second two tugs, I'll let the line go slack. You tie it to the trigger, and then . . ."

"Skedaddle." Paloma had the picture.

"Okay guys, see you in a couple of hours." I stuck the rest of the duct tape into my shirt, took the end of the line, and crawled away along the brush pile toward the mine. I tried to keep the line straight, but when I looked back after a couple of hundred feet I could see it touching trees on both sides. The line was nice and smooth though, and it continued to pull right along.

I felt as if I had crawled at least two thousand feet and had about decided that Renaldo had let the line get away from him, or maybe it had broken somewhere. I was seriously thinking that maybe I should turn back to check, and that was a bad thought because the sun was getting right along down toward the treetops and any afternoon charters should be showing up pretty soon.

I heard a familiar whir through the trees. An airplane had drifted down, power off, and I heard it bounce down on the runway. I was having original thoughts about the best laid plans of mice and men when Renaldo gave me two nice long tugs on the line. I stopped and gave him two tugs back. He tugged again, at least once more, maybe twice. I let the line go slack and waited.

The airplane bumped and creaked to a stop, almost directly across the brush pile from me, and then I couldn't believe my ears. The pilot gave one engine a shot of power to turn the plane around, and it was the unmistakable, deep-throated growl of a nine-cylinder radial. I'd have been just as surprised, but a heck of a lot happier, to hear the whine of a turbine, or better yet a small jet.

The thing is, no one has made a nine cylinder radial since WWII. There are plenty of them still around, every one of them still flying on the slush pile of engines that were surplused at the end of WWII. One rumor had it that some guy in Hawaii bought 2,000 new Pratt and Whitney Wasps still in their shipping crates. Supposedly they cost him ten dollars apiece, with the proviso that he move them off of government property within 48 hours.

Those were not bad engines. In fact, they were pretty wonderful and played a major role in winning that war. What happened to them when the first jet screamed into existence was the same thing that happened to the best generation of draft horses the world had ever known when a Model T Ford truck chuckled and clanked over the horizon.

I tied the line to a tree, leaving plenty of slack in it, and crawled through the brush to see if Renaldo had chartered a Fokker Tri-motor, or maybe an American Pilgrim. It wasn't quite that bad. The plane sitting in the center of the field fifty feet from me was a Beech 18. That was a luxury airliner in its day, only its day was in the 1930s. I was admiring the numerous patches on the fuselage and tail when the door dropped open and the pilot stepped out to sit on the steps and smoke.

He fit my idea of an old codger. A thick tangle of white hair stuck out under a baseball cap, and he wore a gray coverall suit, more like a mechanic than a pilot. Considering what he was flying, he was probably both. I wondered about my chance of taking him right then. He had a sidearm strapped in a holster on his hip, but he wasn't expecting trouble. If I shot at him and missed, the bullets would punch out through the other side of the fuselage and the holes wouldn't even be noticeable on that patched-up tin can.

Maybe it was professional courtesy, pilot to pilot, but I hesitated, and a pickup truck bumped out of the lane onto the runway. There must have been eight guys sitting in the bed of that truck and three more in the cab. Over half of them were holding some kind of automatic weapon. I eased into the brush and inched backward toward the line.

The first thing I had to do was shed my crawling suit, and that was a pure pleasure. The next project was to work the line over to the edge of the runway without pulling on it. I untied the line from my tree and worked back thirty feet, coiling the line in my hand as I went. I found a nice smooth tree to pull the line around like a pulley and backed toward the runway, uncoiling the line again.

I wondered how long it had been since Renaldo tied off the line, and how far he and Paloma had crawled in case I made a mistake. I decided they were probably half way back to the end of the runway by now, or at least plenty far from the bomb to survive the blast. All the same, I was one careful kid uncoiling that line through the brush pile until I could peek out through leaves and see the runway while still holding the line.

Men were piling out of the truck. I lay on the ground, imagining squirrels and rabbits, or South American versions of same, chewing the line in two, or dozens of monkeys picking up the line to play with it. Meanwhile, I watched the men around the pickup truck. It turned out that most of the men were guards, surrounding the airplane with guns at the ready while only two guys tossed the bags out of the truck into the airplane.

A second truck bumped out of the woods and lined up behind the first. I looked around for the pilot and saw his white thatch through the cockpit window. Four guys jumped out of the second pickup and joined the unloaders. I guessed that was about as much confusion as there was apt to be, and the second pickup surely held all the rest of the shipment.

I pulled on the line. It came easily, so I pulled more. Line was piling up around me and I was sure that either something had cut it, or Renaldo's knot had come untied. There was nothing else to do, so I kept pulling line, getting a vision of the bomb pulling right along and suddenly popping around my tree into my lap. The line came tight and wouldn't budge. I gave it a jerk, wondering just how hard one can pull on a ten-pound test line. Well, it's pretty hard.

Suddenly the line moved two inches, and the jungle let out a bellow like Krakatoa. Trees bent down and whipped with the blast, and a blessed dust cloud whiffed up the runway and covered everything. I ran half way to the airplane before

I could see men milling around. They seemed to be of two minds. Some were running toward the blast waving guns, others were running away from the blast, back toward the mine.

I stopped running, but strode purposefully to the first truck, grabbed up a sack and shoved my way through the crowd of gawkers into the airplane. A couple of guys got the idea and followed me in with sacks. I noticed that I didn't have to worry about being gringo. All of us were the same shade of white dust. For Juan's sake, I hoped it was more bauxite.

Sacks were stacked toward the front of the cabin in the remnants of a cargo net, but several had been dropped just inside the door. I jumped up into the airplane and started grabbing the bags by the door and carrying them forward. Bags were suddenly coming in fast, so I was running and tossing to catch up. When a lull came, I carried the last bag all the way up to the cockpit and slammed it down in the co-pilot's seat.

The pilot had been watching out through his window. When he spun around he found my .357 two inches from his nose. He threw up his hands and very wisely clamped his mouth shut. I had the roll of tape ready in my other hand and started with his mouth before he changed his mind. I kept right on wrapping over his eyes, leaving a red Santa Claus nose sticking out, but otherwise I mummified him right up to the baseball cap.

Once his eyes were covered, I jammed the gun back in my belt and jerked his arms down. I didn't want anyone to notice his posture, but no one was paying any attention to the cockpit. I taped his hands behind him with a dozen wraps of tape and shoved him down in the little space between the pilot's seat and the bulkhead. He sat down willingly enough. I took off his baseball cap and jammed it on my head, gave his ankles a couple of wraps, and sat down in the pilot's seat.

Someone else had climbed into the cabin to pile the sacks, and the sacks were coming in double time. A couple of guys were running back from the direction of the blast, waving their guns in the air, and the general idea seemed to be to get that plane loaded and out of there fast. That was fine with me.

I tried to remember how many years it had been since I'd flown a Beech 18, and rejected the answer when it came, because I didn't think I was that old. I was looking for the master switch when my hand reached out and flipped it. That's the true meaning of *body memory*. Your body knows things that your mind has forgotten.

The cabin door slammed shut, and the pickups pulled away from the plane. A white-dusted guy was standing in front of me making frantic "fly away" motions. My hand automatically went to the wobble pump beside the copilot's seat, so I gave it a couple of strokes to pressurize the fuel system. I gave the left engine four shots of the primer and hit the starter. The starter whined, the prop spun, but the engine had no interest in starting.

I finally remembered that the last time I started a nine-cylinder radial it was ten below zero. I had used way too much prime for a hot engine, and flooded it. I jerked the mixture control lean to cut off the gasoline, opened the throttle wide to get some serious air into the cylinders, and kept on cranking. Another endless twenty seconds crawled by before a cylinder fired.

I jerked the throttle back and the next cylinder fired, which wasn't so unusual. Those old radials always start one cylinder at a time, with a lengthy pause between, but once that crankshaft is turning over under power, nothing can stop it. I jammed the mixture control rich again, and the bang . . . bang . . . became bang, bang.

The left engine smoothed out, and the alternator needle jumped up against the pin. I had darn near drained the battery. I let it charge for ten seconds and cranked the right engine without priming. It sprang to instant life as though it had never been shut off. The guy in front of me was waving me on so I cracked the throttles, and he dived off to the side.

I bumped and creaked down the runway, just a little faster than a fast walk, but I was busy remembering where to set the trim and how much flap to use for takeoff. A yellow switch next to the column was made to look like a flap. When I laid my hand on it, I automatically pushed it down fifteen degrees so I guessed that was right.

Maybe when Beech made the 18, they didn't quite trust electricity yet. The flaps and landing gear were controlled by electric motors, but the hand crank was right beside my seat. Push it in and it cranks down flaps, pull it out and it cranks the landing gear up or down. The electricity worked fine. The flaps lowered to the same position as the switch.

The controls were smooth. The gasoline switch was on the left main tank, and it was full. Both engines showed sixty pounds of oil pressure, which seemed pretty good for hot engines in the tropics. I didn't bother checking magnetos or feathering props. With the trucks full of guns behind me, I wasn't about to stop and change any spark plugs or oil filters. I was still running my mental checklist when I came to the end of the runway and spun the plane around.

I stopped just a little short of turning all the way around so the loading door was hidden from the other end of the runway. The pickups had retreated off to the sides, but they looked like pin cushions with all the guns sticking up. I set the brake and jerked the pilot out of his niche. He seemed to be all cooperation, so I used my penknife to cut the tape between his ankles. I helped him over the pile of bags and opened the door.

Renaldo and Paloma came bursting out of the brush, Renaldo clutching the money bag. Paloma beat Renaldo to the plane by ten yards and leapt inside. Renaldo tossed the money bag in, and I tossed the pilot out. Renaldo caught him, looked a little surprised, and laid him down on the ground. Renaldo vaulted in, I jerked the chain to slam the door and locked the latch. I dived back into the pilot's seat and opened the throttles.

I got the expected roar, like thunder rolling down concrete stairs. The frame creaked appropriately, adjusting itself to the torque. What I didn't get was the sinking-into-the-seat sensation of sudden acceleration. I was checking things fast. Brake was off, props on low pitch, manifold pressure was 37 inches, and both engines were turning 2600 rpm.

That might not sound like much if you're used to zipping around in your Beamer with the engine turning three times that fast, but for those old radials, swinging eight-foot Hamilton Standard props, 2600 is well over red line. The gauges said we were developing over 1,000 horsepower out of two engines rated 450 each.

We were accelerating all right, but nothing like I expected. I tried calculating load, and didn't have much handle on it, but there couldn't be over a ton of cocaine back there, no problem for this old workhorse. We'd used up half the runway, and the airspeed indicator said 50. Nothing to do but stay on full power and pray, because if I tried to stop now we'd be in the trees anyhow, with twenty automatic rifles checking on us.

I dumped the flaps to get rid of the last bit of drag and concentrated on holding our angle of attack neutral so we were gaining speed with no useless lift wasting power. We passed 65 mph with less than 1,000 feet of runway left, and both engines were at red line for oil temperature.

"Hey, aren't we supposed to fly or something?" Renaldo hollered. He was right beside my ear, but with those Pratt and Whitney Wasps tearing their guts out, I barely heard him.

"Don't worry about it," I hollered back. "If we hit the trees with this load, you'll be stoned for the rest of your life."

We touched 70 miles per, and I was looking up at the trees. I slammed down the flap switch a full twenty degrees, hit the gear retract, and hauled back on the column. We ballooned up over the trees, but lost speed in the process. I dived down to cross the hundred-yard clearing at the mine and got back a little airspeed. We were hanging steady, barely missing the treetops, and the oil temperature was climbing right on up, past the red line and into the "bail out now" zone. The needles on the cylinder head temperature gauges had disappeared to the right.

The canyon was two hundred yards off to our right, and I fudged over toward it, but didn't dare bank. We couldn't spare the lift. I wasn't judging our imminent stall by the airspeed indicator. I was judging the stall because it felt as if we were flying in molasses, and the controls seemed to be connected by old rubber bands instead of steel rods and bell cranks.

RPM on the right engine started to fall off. It was just too hot. With fifty feet to go to the edge of the canyon, we clipped the first tree. There's a terrible temptation to raise the nose and try to fly over things, but with no airspeed, that would have been fatal. If we'd lost even two miles per hour, we'd have pancake stalled, straight down and deadly. In that situation, you're better off to fly straight ahead and hit whatever you're going to hit rather than to stall. We were settling down into the treetops when we blasted over the rim of the canyon. I dropped the nose down into all that glorious air below us, and backed off the power from flat out full emergency to a high cruise.

Speed built up fast and I raised the flaps. The engines cooled down to respectable, and with an airspeed of a hundred-fifty knots, we soared back up out of the canyon and turned north toward the gap in the mountains. I finally had time to look around. Paloma was sitting in the copilot's seat, Renaldo was kneeling between us, and both of them looked pale through the dirt on their faces. It was probably a good thing I couldn't see myself.

"Gee, not much like the tri-pacer, huh?" Paloma asked.

"Well, it should have been. Something is terribly wrong, and I can't figure out what. Every gauge said we had full power, but it just wasn't there."

"Well, we're up now. It doesn't matter any more now, does it?" Renaldo asked.

"Maybe not. We'll clear the mountains, and after that we can just follow the coast, but I wish I knew what was wrong."

"What do you mean, follow the coast?" Renaldo asked.

"Well, not exactly follow it, but we should have enough fuel to reach Panama City. We'll need a lighted runway, so it's pretty much right up the coast anyway."

"These flights usually go straight to Miami. They fly all night and land on a dirt strip right outside Ft. Lauderdale."

"They what?"

"They fly straight to Florida. What's so hard about that?"

"Nothing, if you don't mind swimming the last five hundred miles. This bird carries just over 270 gallons of fuel. That gives it a maximum range of one thousand miles and change." The truth suddenly dawned.

"Paloma, hold the yoke right there. I'm going to walk to the back, and the plane is going to try to climb, so push down a little and keep the horizon right where it is on the windshield." I got up to slide past Renaldo. He sat down in my seat, and I climbed back over the pile of white bags. The rear bulkhead was right behind the loading door. I opened the door in the bulkhead and there was the little chemical toilet. Did I mention that this was one classy airliner in its day?

I suddenly realized I was bending over to walk through the cabin. I used to walk through the cabin in a Beech 18 standing upright, and I hadn't grown taller lately. The entire roof of that cabin was a steel fuel tank. A fuel gauge and a valve were mounted on the bulkhead right behind the pilot's seat. The gauge read *full* and the stencil beside it read: *500 gals. 100/130.* I was looking at over 4,000 pounds that I hadn't known was there. If I'd known, I'd have turned onto the runway under full power with no flaps, and concentrated on gaining speed instead of checking everything in the cockpit.

However, now that we were up, more by luck than good management, I was looking at ten hours of extra flying time. With that auxiliary tank and a full load in the mains, we had a range of over 3,100 miles. We could darn near make Miami and back, even if we made a legal detour around Cuban airspace.

I worked my way up front and made a seat-shaped pile of bags between the pilots' seats. I sat down on the bags and settled in nice and comfy.

"Paloma," I said, "roll us 45 degrees to the right and hold it there. We're going to Miami, and if the weather in Miami is bad, we'll go to New York."

Chapter 23

"Paloma, see that black wheel between the columns?"

"This one?"

"Yeah. Roll it toward you until the airspeed drops ten knots. At the same time, watch the little white airplane in the artificial horizon, yeah, that one. It'll come up about one line-width above the solid line so hold it there."

"How can I watch two things at once, and what are we doing, anyway?"

"Hey, you wanted to learn to fly. You've got to practice being shifty-eyed. We're climbing up to ten thousand feet. We'll be faster and burn less fuel. Renaldo, dig around in that map case and find a chart of the Caribbean."

Paloma climbed, but Renaldo found the case empty. "Check the jockey box. Maybe the door pouches?"

Renaldo dug, calmly at first, and then with the urgency

that I was beginning to feel. There were no charts in that aircraft. The old pilot had made this trip so many times the charts were in his head. Unfortunately, his head was left on the runway.

Renaldo shrugged and tried to look unconcerned. "No problem, right? You do know your way around?"

"We're just a little out of my territory, but North America should be hard to miss. I think a heading of about three hundred-fifty degrees should hit Florida."

"You *think*? *About*?"

"Close enough for government work. Turn on that radio, no, the lower one. See the arrow beside it? All we have to do is tune in a Miami station. The arrow points toward it, and we follow, no problem."

Renaldo turned on the radio, and static filled the cockpit. He tuned slowly across the dial, nothing but static. The automatic direction finder needle spun slowly around, just a little slower than the second hand on a clock.

"The little short wide hand is on one," Paloma announced. "Does that mean ten thousand feet?"

"That it does. Crank the wheel back down until the little airplane is sitting on the horizon line."

"Are we too far away to receive Miami?" Renaldo asked.

"Maybe, but that's not the problem. That's Lake Maracaibo below us, we're approaching the coastline ahead. We should be receiving half a dozen stations from Caracas and another dozen from wherever. The problem is supposed to be picking out the right station, not finding a station to begin with."

"You mean the radio's broken?"

"Seems like. No big problem. We're on dead reckoning, that's all."

Renaldo turned around to scowl at me. "I don't think I like the sound of *dead*."

"Hey, oldest method of navigation known to man. People have been circumnavigating the globe with dead reckoning for five hundred years. You travel at a certain speed on a known heading for a certain length of time, and you will be at a certain place."

"Good, and you think that heading is *about* three hundred-fifty degrees? How much time, *about*?"

"Maybe seven or eight hours. You'll recognize Florida, it's long and thin. Meanwhile, we should fly right over Jamaica in a couple of hours. We'll use the lights of Kingston to correct our course a little if we have to."

Paloma turned around. She didn't scowl, but she didn't look very happy. "Glad to hear there'll be lights in Kingston Town. I see an awful lot of ocean ahead of us, and that looks very much like a sunset on the left."

"As it should. Sunset in the west, we're flying north, can't go wrong." I was a little surprised though. The sunset was behind the wing, and with a three hundred-fifty degree heading, it should have been on the wingtip, or slightly ahead. Still, I was barely in my hemisphere, and the exact location of sunsets changes with the seasons. I hadn't bothered to check Renaldo's almanac. Seemed like we were close to the fall equinox, so the sun should be over the equator, but I decided not to worry. The sky turned orange, the ocean magenta. The sun dipped into some high clouds that I hoped were over Panama, made purple streaks, turned the edge of the clouds to gold, then disappeared and sucked the light with it.

"Getting kinda dark, isn't it?" Paloma asked.

"No problem. See that row of toggle switches along the bottom of the dash? Just flip them up and we'll have lots of light."

I held my breath while Paloma flipped switches, but the third one produced a warm red glow on the instrument panel, just a little brighter than the sunset. Then there wasn't any sunset, and the only light in the universe was our instrument panel.

"Now what?" Paloma asked.

"Now, nothing. Just keep the little airplane level and keep the compass steady. Check our airspeed every twenty seconds and mention if it changes."

"Right, and I'm supposed to do that for how many hours?"

"We'll take turns. By the way, there's a powder room in back in case anyone wants to wash their face."

We did take turns, both flying and face washing. A dim overhead light came on in the bathroom when the door closed, so that was one of the toggles Paloma had switched. Naturally, Renaldo went first and came out looking pristine. Paloma followed, but the water in the sink stopped running, leaving Renaldo clean, Paloma half and half, and me filthy.

Paloma borrowed my pocket comb and worked on her hair for twenty minutes while Renaldo watched the artificial horizon. With the right side of her face clean and the left side still jungle covered, she looked like a rock star. She'd been far enough from the blast that her extraneous coloring was mostly black from the jungle. I was still covered with the white dust, so the six-inch square polished steel mirror in the head showed a Kabuki dancer. I tried wiping off dust with toilet tissue, but it felt like sandpaper so I let it stay.

Nothing else happened for an eternity except that my watch seemed to slow down. The steady roar of those nine-cylinder radials was a solid, dependable sound, and after a while your ears go numb so the level is tolerable. When I took my turn in the pilot's seat, I found the knob under the light switch and dimmed the panel so we could see some stars. I was hoping to spot the big dipper and get a real fix on north, but it was lost in the haze. The sky wasn't overcast, but the stars looked smeary and murky, and there was no hint of anything below us.

A light finally grew out of the ocean and gradually turned into a city, but it was off to our right. It was a half hour later than I thought it should be, but that had only been a wild guess. I corrected to fly over it, and we strained to identify anything, but it was just an amorphous blob.

"Is that Kingston?" Paloma asked.

"What else could it be? We were only a couple of degrees off. Let's correct to three fifty-two and in an hour or so we'll see Cuba. Probably lights at Guantanamo. Renaldo, hold the yoke. Time to refill the gas tank."

I climbed back past Paloma and turned on the valve next to the gauge on the bulkhead. For a minute nothing happened, and I was looking around for life preservers, but finally the gauge started down. I leaned into the cockpit and watched the fuel level in the main tanks come up. I closed the valve at three quarters, no point in taking a chance of overflow.

An hour crept by, then two. No lights on Cuba, but maybe there shouldn't be. Cuba is depressed and desperate, so maybe they don't light streets at night. Gradually the sky began to lighten, the stars went out, and a carpet spread out below us with white speckles here and there on gray waves.

The sky turned orange, then tinted the speckles, and we were seeing an ocean. Lots and lots of ocean, and no land in sight. When the sun finally peeked a red ball out of the waves, it was ahead of the right wing, and not just a little bit.

"I suppose Miami is just over the horizon?" Renaldo asked.

"Well, you know, that might be a problem. We can see about fifty miles, and I had the impression there should be islands around."

Paloma was scanning the horizon, using her hand to block the sun from her eyes. "Certainly no islands out there, so what went wrong?"

"What's wrong is the compass. We haven't turned, but maybe the compass is four or five degrees off."

"How can that be?" Paloma asked. "We were almost on course when we went over Kingston."

"Yeah, that's what I thought. Come on, you guys know the Caribbean, what the devil happened?"

"Bermuda Triangle?" Renaldo wondered.

"Not without some islands around. Come on, think."

Paloma was thinking, judging by the furrow in her half-clean forehead. "Maybe that wasn't Kingston. If the compass was off, it could have been Port-Au-Prince on Haiti. Then we turned more to the right, so that explains why no Cuba. We might be in the middle of the Atlantic Ocean."

"Well, not the middle just yet, but we're headed that way. According to the sun, we're headed ten degrees west of north, and the sun is pretty reliable." I banked left until the sun was directly behind us. The compass should have read two hundred-seventy, it read two-sixty.

"Okay, children, compass off ten degrees. No problem

if you know it, little rough if you don't. I think we can rely on the sun, and we'd better. If we're wrong, if we're in the Gulf of Mexico, we may end up swimming yet."

Renaldo had developed a perpetual scowl. "If the compass is off, how come the regular pilot flies straight to Florida?"

"Because he knew the compass was off and allowed for it. He just neglected to mention it when I took over."

A long hour passed. I went back and refilled the gas tank. The auxiliary tank read empty, the mains three quarters full. The sun got higher. We kept the shadow of our tail on the cowling.

"Land ho!" Renaldo shouted. He was pointing toward a little green dot of an island on the left. It wasn't much, a couple of palm trees surrounded by mangrove, certainly not a place to land, but it was encouraging. In ten more minutes the smooth maritime horizon had bumps on it, and suddenly islands were everywhere. We still had half tanks of fuel, so I let myself believe we might survive.

"Recognize anything?" I asked Paloma.

"I think that big one on the right might be Grand Bahama. It's about the right shape, and it's running east and west."

"Great, where does that put us?"

"Well, I think we're a bit north of Miami, but like you said, Florida is long and thin so it should be hard to miss."

She was right. In another half hour, a solid coastline stretched ahead of us. That's when the two fighter jets came screaming down and locked onto our wingtips.

"What the devil do they want?" Renaldo asked.

"We're on somebody's radar and we haven't called in. They think we're drug smugglers."

"That's ridiculous." Renaldo gave a haughty sniff.

"Yeah? And just what's in those bags Paloma's sitting on?"

"Damn, that could be a problem, couldn't it?"

I had a good view of the pilots on both sides of us, and both of them were pointing down and to the left. They looked like spacemen in their flying gear, no faces visible, but their hand gestures were pretty clear. I waved and nodded, and we turned left in formation. They were pointing down, rather vehemently, and crowding us. Their wingtips were just above ours so they screwed up our lift anyway, and I had the impression they might shove us down if we didn't comply. Just beyond the beach, houses and buildings concentrated into a town with a good-sized airport. I nodded to the pilot on my left, backed off power and dived. If the jets had been any closer, they'd have rubbed off paint.

"Anyone know what town that is?"

Paloma was scanning the beach, taking in landmarks, I suppose, but the terrain beyond was flat enough to play pool. "Either Fort Lauderdale or Opalocka . . . probably Fort Lauderdale."

"Good enough, maybe it doesn't matter. See that stretch of beach with the trees beside the highway?"

Renaldo was looking around, but not happily. I had a sudden fear that he'd give the pilot on his side the finger. "Yeah, so?"

"So, tighten your seat belt. Paloma, go back and brace yourself against the bulkhead. I'm going to land with the gear up and we're going to stop as if we'd hit a brick wall."

We'd been diving at a hundred sixty knots toward the airport, and the jets were staying with us, but they were looking wobbly. I judged we were close to their stalling speed.

At one thousand feet, I chopped the power, jammed the flaps all the way down, and jerked the nose up. We almost stopped in mid air and the jets flashed ahead of us. Hard left bank, hard right rudder, we stalled and spun. The plane dropped like the rock it was, slamming Renaldo against his window and eliciting something like profanity from Paloma. I let two spins go by and we were down to two hundred feet. Straighten the rudder, touch of power on the port engine, level the wings, and we pulled out over the beach.

Renaldo was braced against the cowling, Paloma was behind the bulkhead and the profanity stopped. I pulled the mixture controls lean to kill the engines, flipped off the master switch. We were skimming over soft sand. Haul the yoke all the way back and brace against the rudder pedals. Everything disappeared in a shower of sand, and my belt tried to cut me in half. The bags of cocaine ripped loose from their webbing and cascaded into the cockpit. Suddenly everything stopped.

I was trying to climb over cocaine bags, like swimming up a waterfall, and Renaldo climbed right over my back. I jerked the cargo door open but it was sitting on sand so the door only opened half way, and I had to squeeze past it. Paloma was right behind me, but no Renaldo.

"Hey, come on. The flights over, good time to leave."

His answer was muffled. "Bags on top the cash. Can't leave without it."

Good point. I scrambled back in. Renaldo was tossing bags, burrowing like a badger. I joined him and bags were flying. He found the briefcase handle, gave a tug, and jerked it free. He beat me to the door.

Paloma was crouched down at the edge of sand dunes thirty feet away. She jumped up and led the way. Renaldo and I followed her, but the dunes were covered with some kind of plants that wrapped our feet, and behind every dune the sand was so soft we sank in a foot. In fifty feet, Paloma flopped on her face panting. Renaldo and I joined her. The sand was gritty and cool, smelling vaguely of raw sewage, but after twelve hours on a moving platform with water underneath it felt good.

Chapter 24

It had seemed quiet when we climbed out of the plane, but then you're always half deaf after those nine-cylinder Wasps pound your head for a few hours. When we stopped panting and looked around we saw people running and shouting from everywhere.

A hundred feet away, on either side of us, wooden bridges spanned the dunes. Those looked like the Boston marathon with pedestrians rushing toward the beach. We were sitting up trying to look inconspicuous when we heard sirens on the road, coming from both directions, and then a cop car slued onto the sand a half mile to our left and came racing along the edge of the waves.

"Good time to leave," Paloma suggested.

We stayed low and picked our way around the dunes. That worked better than running. We came to the stand of bamboo at the edge of the dunes without attracting attention, but a six-foot wooden fence blocked us. Beyond the fence a four-story building, roughly shaped like a ship, appeared to be condominiums.

Paloma and I grabbed the top of the fence and chinned ourselves to look over. Renaldo was bouncing on his toes, he couldn't let go of the bag. Beyond the fence was a courtyard, with white plastic furniture surrounding a swimming pool.

"Let's go." I grabbed one of Paloma's feet, Renaldo grabbed the other, and we boosted her to the top of the fence. She sat on it, spun around, and dropped. Renaldo tossed the bag over. I bent down to make a stirrup of my hands for Renaldo, but he stepped on my back and scrambled over. The world seemed to be wrapped in sirens, all blending into Gabriel's final trump. I skinned over that wall as if it had been a ladder.

We had the courtyard all to ourselves. Paloma and I knelt beside the pool. She washed her face; I just stuck my head under and swished it around like rinsing a mop. I stood up, shaking like a wet dog. Paloma grabbed my shirt, unbuttoned it, and pulled my tee shirt up. She wiped her face on that, so I did too, and used my comb to swish a quart of water out of my hair. A middle-aged woman who looked Mexican bounded up some concrete steps from a basement. She dropped a laundry basket beside the pool and ran to open a gate at the end of the fence. She didn't even glance at us. Ten seconds later, she appeared sprinting across the walkway toward the beach.

"Shall we hide in the laundry room?" Renaldo suggested.

I had to wait to answer until some frantic blasts on an air horn subsided, probably one of those articulated fire trucks, in case the wreck was several stories tall. It was blatting like a diesel switch engine at a crossing.

As soon as I could hear, I shouted. "No, I think we should take a lesson from Edgar Allen Poe. Remember *The Purloined Letter?*"

Renaldo furrowed his brow. "Now that you mention it, no. So?"

"It's a classic, so I probably have it wrong, but roughly a bunch of cops are tossing an apartment looking for a missing letter. They jerk out drawers, look under and behind them, rip down light fixtures, whatever, searching all the clever places where a letter could be hidden. Meanwhile, the letter is in plain sight on the dining room table mixed with the incoming mail."

"You think we should hide on a dining room table?"

"No, I think the cops will surround the area, rip down the bamboo, and take the condos apart, looking for people trying to run or hide. I think we should stroll down to the beach and see what all the excitement is about."

Paloma nodded and led the way. We stepped through the gate into a street that ended at the dunes and connected with the walkway toward the beach. The other end of the street, a hundred feet to our right, was blocked by cop cars, fire trucks, and army trucks, all jammed nose to nose. Not only were cops milling around chasing away cars that threatened to turn in, but a solid line of National Guard, wearing khaki and brandishing automatic rifles, had formed a perimeter. We turned the other way and joined late arrivals scurrying toward what appeared to be a carnival on the beach. Our fellow gawkers were wearing everything from bathing suits to pajamas so we fit right in.

The beach looked like downtown Baghdad with Humvees, half-tracks, and cop cars surrounding the airplane.

National Guardsmen with rifles were standing shoulder to shoulder, threatening to shoot the crowd. An ambulance screamed onto the beach and slued toward us through the ruts. It stopped next to a knot of shouting people who were distracted from the plane. Medics jumped out of the ambulance, scooped a body onto a stretcher, slapped an oxygen mask on it, and loaded it. A little old man followed the stretcher. Doors closed, siren screamed, and the ambulance raced back down the beach. I joined that crowd and found a woman in pink bathing cap, blue bikini, and green robe who didn't appear hysterical.

"Victim from the crash?" I asked.

"No, heart attack. There's a dozen dead bodies inside the airplane, but they haven't brought them out yet."

The crowd at the heart attack site dispersed and joined the mob around the airplane, jockeying for positions to see the bodies. An armored car pulled onto the beach and immediately sank to its bumpers in the sand. A National Guard half-track sputtered to life, several guards jumped in and it raced to rescue the stricken vehicle. Men milled around the truck while a cable was attached. The half-track dug itself into the sand and strained. The front bumper ripped off the armored truck, slammed the back of the halftrack. The cable had cut a wide swath, and several men were left lying on the sand. They reminded me of the carnage that Juan Junior had wreaked with his imaginary machine gun.

The crowd was torn between waiting to see the bodies coming out of the airplane or running down the beach to inspect the bodies laid low by the cable. Only about ten percent deserted. More ambulances came, this time army-colored with red crosses on the sides. We stayed with the larger crowd, but it appeared that about half the new ambulances were also stuck. Then I noticed that the tide was coming in, and waves were reaching the armored car.

Important looking men in civilian clothes climbed in and out of the plane, some carrying clip boards, others shouting at walkie-talkies, none carrying bodies. The crowd was getting restless; mutinous murmurs spread. A wrecker arrived at the scene of ambulances and armored truck, put down stabilizers, and winched ambulances onto firmer sand. They cranked up sirens and raced away. An operator in hip boots waded out to the armored truck, attached his cable, and pulled it out backward. The doors were open, apparently the crew had deserted. Water ran out of the passenger door. The wrecker retracted stabilizers, shortened the cable, and towed the armored car away backward. Spectators trudged back to join us in our fruitless vigil.

A young Mexican entrepreneur came pushing a steam cart across the bridge. He stopped short of bouncing it down the steps, but he was instantly surrounded. He was the answer to the most urgent problem we had. My stomach did a flip and grated against my backbone.

We deserted the airplane to fight our way into the crowd around the vendor, procured two hot dogs and a Coke each, and rejoined the mob while we scarfed them down. Nothing like a twenty-four-hour hiatus to make food appetizing. Those hot dogs were superb, right down to the relish that I licked off the waxed paper.

The term, *safety in numbers*, had taken on real significance for us, so when the crowd began to give up and drift away, we joined a group of about thirty people who were muttering their disappointment and trudging back to the walkway.

Cops met us at the cross street, rebuffed those who tried to cross, and herded us onto the sidewalk, waving us toward town with their nightsticks. We obediently marched the first block in a group. People began splitting off; some crossed the street and headed back, a few ducked into buildings. We were down to ten people when the cadre streamed up a flight of wooden stairs into an open beachside bar.

We found a vacant table next to the railing that overlooked the street. It was shady and cool after the vigil on the beach, and a big overhead fan lazily stirred a welcome breeze. A menu on the table suggested a sampler platter and listed every delicacy that's ever come out of the Atlantic Ocean. A pert blonde waitress wearing shorts, halter, and cowboy boots brought water and poised with a pen and pad. We ordered the sampler. Renaldo wanted gin and tonic, and Paloma ordered a glass of the house white, which turned out to be a California Riesling. To celebrate our arrival in Florida, I ordered a piña colada as a breakfast milkshake. The waitress nodded and ran, we attacked the water.

"What's the next plan?" Paloma asked.

I shrugged. "What would you like to do? Our little caper seems to be over, so maybe it's time to split up. As singles we're pretty safe, as a trio we could be suspicious." I made that a casual remark, but I did feel more than a twinge of loss at parting ways with Paloma.

She nodded. "Yeah, I was thinking that. Mother's family is in California. They'll welcome me with open arms, and they don't carry guns."

"You'll need money," Renaldo said, and reached toward the briefcase between his feet. The waitress appeared and set down a steaming platter of deep-fried mysteries, along with a check in a pseudo leather wallet. Renaldo was still reaching toward the briefcase. I slapped his hand and put my American Express card on the check. The waitress scooped it up and disappeared again.

"Renaldo, my lad, we're in the United States now, so do what the natives do. Pay for everything with a credit card. If you pull out a bundle of hundred-dollar bills here, like to check into a hotel for instance, you'll find the IRS, the DEA, the ATF, the FBI, and every other acronym under the flag waiting for you in the hotel room. In the good old U.S. of A., that suitcase full of cash is as serious a federal crime as the cocaine was."

Renaldo nodded, but he opened the bag anyway and passed bundles of bills under the table to Paloma until she stopped him.

"Hold it, enough is a enough. All I want is a coast-to-coast ticket, and I've had enough flying for a while. I'm taking a Greyhound. Alex is right. Mother's family charges everything and uses old dirty hundred-dollar bills to line birdcages. I really don't need money."

He shrugged and turned to me. "Alex?"

I was in serious trouble. I'd picked up what appeared to be an oyster, bitten it in half, and it was so hot my tongue was sizzling. I doused the fire with the piña colada and gasped for a moment before I could answer him. "I need to get back to work. The Kuskokwim River will be freezing up, and that's our busiest time. There's too much ice for the natives to travel by boat, not enough for snow machines, and everyone is trying to get done what they should have done all summer. Vickie will be so busy she'll be glad to see me, and might even forget to read me the riot act."

Renaldo nodded again and passed me two bundles under the table. I stuffed them into my pocket and assumed they were ten thousand each. Probably enough to cover my American Express bill. I approached the oyster more judiciously, and it was even better than the hot dogs on the beach.

"What are you going to do?" I asked Renaldo.

He had picked up a crab leg, deep fried and battered, but nibbled to test it before he bit. "I'm thinking I'll head for Las Vegas. That's the one town in the U.S. where a suitcase full of cash is legal tender."

We finished the platter and the drinks and suddenly got very quiet. It was dawning on us that the party was over. We stood and grabbed each other in a long, desperate, three-way hug. When we stepped apart, we were smiling, but tears were running down Paloma's cheeks, and my eyes were a little misty too.

Paloma turned resolutely around, did a deep knee bend, and swung her way out of the bar doing a cha cha. Renaldo and I exchanged shrugs and saluted each other. He picked up the briefcase, used it for a partner, and launched into a spirited mambo through the bar and down the steps.

I blinked my eyes a couple of times, took a swipe at them with my handkerchief, and waltzed my way out to the first cabstand.

~The End~

About the Author

After a childhood in the big woods outside Seattle, Don Porter absorbed a modicum of education at a junior college in Iowa and went to Alaska in 1954 to seek his fortune and pursue an engineering degree at the University of Alaska in Fairbanks.

He never finished that degree because during his senior year he was licensed by the F.C.C. and became the Chief Engineer of KFAR-AM and KFAR-TV in Fairbanks, part of the Midnight Sun Network that covered the entire state. He spent the next twenty years building stations all over Alaska—literally, from cable in Ketchikan, Point Barrow, Nome, Cordova, and Kodiak to broadcast stations in Anchorage, Fairbanks, Juneau, Sitka—you get the idea. Midnight Sun also blanketed the rural areas with mountaintop repeaters.

Midway through that fiasco, time and troubles forced the engineering staff to fly between sites. The company rented the aircraft; Don flew them. After twenty years in broadcasting, and with a commercial pilot's license and five thousand hours in the air, he gave up electronics to become a bush pilot.

He flew charter based in Bethel on the Yukon-Kuskokwim Delta for the next fifteen years and picked up ratings for multi-engine, instrument, and helicopter. If it has an airfoil and an engine, he has probably flown it. Passengers were state troopers, mothers in labor, dead bodies, wedding parties, whatever. On the Delta, Eskimos outnumber Gussaks about ten to one. He was steeped in, and came to respect, the Eskimo culture.

Because of his jobs he covered Alaska from Ketchikan to Point Barrow and from Tok to the tip of the Aleutian Chain. He also grubstaked prospectors. He supplied the expenses and transportation; they dug up the valleys looking for gold. His fifty percent of the profits never paid the gasoline bill.

Back to electronics and two years on Oahu making warranty house calls for Sony. A whirlwind tour of the South Pacific, island hopping and building whatever needed building, including two years on Guam resurrecting KUAM, AM, FM, and TV.

He spent the next fifteen years as Director of Maintenance for the ABC television network throughout Hawaii, living, working, and writing in Honolulu. His wife Deborah is an artist who has calmly painted pictures and made a home wherever they've landed. When word processors made it practical, he started writing books about Alaska and Hawaii.

He now spends six weeks in summer signing books at fairs in Alaska. The Tanana Valley Fair (Fairbanks), the Ninilchik Fair, and the Palmer Fair (Anchorage). Those bracket August and the beginning of September. September and October are the Central Washington State Fairs in Spokane and Yakima. January and February are spent at the craft fairs in Quartzsite, Arizona. The rest of the year he travels most weekends in an ancient but self contained RV signing at fairs, markets, and book stores around Arizona, California, and New Mexico.

Author's Note

The author first landed in La Guara, Venezuela aboard a cruise ship and passengers were supposed to board buses to be whisked away to Caracas. One glance at La Guara, and he ducked out on Caracas. He spent the day exploring La Guara, mostly in open mouthed amazement, and it wasn't nearly enough. For the next several years Venezuela was his vacation destination. It's every bit as spectacular as Alaska, and it's warm.

Housing in La Guara includes structures on a hill so steep that they appear to be stacked. Super rich in walled estates at the bottom and poorer and poorer houses, shacks, hovels, reaching almost straight up for a thousand feet. A power line runs along the bottom of the hill behind the estates. The image that first captivated the author, and that he can still see clearly many years later, is garbage, miscellaneous and one banana peel, hanging in the power lines where the folks on top had been dumping their garbage on the rich.

Don G. Porter

Other books by Don G. Porter
(Not published by Treble Heart)

All available with free shipping from www.dongporter.com

Dick, George, and Maggie, The Hawaiian Detective Agency

The Dealership
Murder Stalks Hawaii
ISBN 978-1-59433-063-6

Murder Pro Bono
Family Matters in Hawaii
ISBN 978-59433-092-6

Jailbird's Daughter
A Payne and Clark Hawaiian Detective Novel
ISBN 978-1-594323-117-6

Set In Alaska featuring Alex Price, bush pilot.

Deadly Detail Trade Paper Back
ISBN 978-1-59058-418-7

Deadly Detail Large Print
ISBN 1-59058-192-X

Happy Hour
ISBN 0-9706712-5-3

Yukon Murders
ISBN 978-0-9706712-9-5

Humpy Cove
ISBN 978-0-9820319-1-9